Southern Biography Series
William J. Cooper, Jr., Editor

RECORDER OF THE
BLACK EXPERIENCE

RECORDER
OF THE BLACK
EXPERIENCE

A Biography of

MONROE NATHAN WORK

Linda O. McMurry

Louisiana State University Press / Baton Rouge and London

Designer: Albert Crochet
Typeface: Linotron Trump Mediaeval
Typesetter: G & S Typesetters, Inc.

Publication of this book has been assisted by a grant
from the Andrew W. Mellon Foundation.

The author gratefully acknowledges the Tuskegee Institute Archives
for permission to reproduce all the photographs herein and to quote
from the materials in the archives.

LIBRARY OF CONGRESS CATALOGING IN PUBLICATION DATA

McMurry, Linda O.
   Recorder of the Black experience.
   (Southern biography series)
   Includes index.
    1. Work Monroe Nathan. 2. Afro-Americans—
Biography. 3. Afro-Americans—Research—History—20th century.
I. Title. II. Series.
E185.97.W79M36 1984   973'.0496024 [B]   84–10008
ISBN 0–8071–1171–6

To the men in my life:
Dad, Richard, Brian, and Jonathan

Contents

Illustrations

Preface

All movements for change depend on individuals who labor quietly for the cause in ways that receive little publicity. Usually such people provide crucial support services for those recognized as the leaders by the media. Monroe Nathan Work was one of these quiet crusaders in the struggle for black rights during the first four decades of the twentieth century.

Neither the nature of Work's activities nor his personality was considered good copy by the press. His research and organizational contributions were not the kind to provoke much interest among the general public. Nothing in his appearance, demeanor, or personality aroused strong emotions. Thus his labors received little attention during his lifetime and afterwards.

Nevertheless, Work and his efforts for justice are significant. He was a pioneer in such areas as African studies, the black health movement, the antilynching crusade, and Afro-American bibliography. Moreover, his life reflects many of the dilemmas confronting black intellectuals in the early twentieth century, dilemmas that have been largely ignored or glossed over by scholars more interested in the battle for black leadership between the two titans W. E. B. Du Bois and Booker T. Washington. The confrontation is indeed interesting, but now, as at the time, scrutiny of it has diverted attention from the basic problems of educated blacks during the period. As the only man to have been closely affiliated with both Du Bois and Washington, Monroe Work is important to the understanding of the complexity of the issues separating the two.

Far too often, historians have seemed to feel compelled to choose sides. Blessed with the luxury of hindsight, most have supported

Du Bois and deprecated Washington's program for black advancement. Few appear to realize that at the turn of the century it was not so easy to see the consequences of either approach. This book is not intended to be an apologia for the accommodationism of Washington. I fully recognize the shortcomings of his policies, but I also believe there has been a tendency to reject the good with the bad. Many individuals have been too freely labeled as either Washingtonians or Niagarans. In the context of the era, men like Work did not find their choices so clear-cut or so mutually exclusive.

My focus is on Work's career rather than his personal life partly because few materials relating to his personal life are available. For almost forty years Work devoted himself to preserving and organizating materials on the black experience. However, he evidently did not consider his own life very important, and there are many gaps in his collected papers. In addition, Work and his career seem to be synonymous. Both his papers and my interviews indicate that he was a relatively simple man who was consumed by his endeavors. His efforts and dreams are therefore more significant than his personality. Finally, I believe that such a focus is what he would have wanted.

I owe a special debt to Jessie P. Guzman, his friend and disciple, for her pioneer article on Work and for the several hours she spent answering my questions on two different occasions. Her dedication to making the truth available rivals that of her mentor.

Others of Work's colleagues, especially Charles Gomillion and Lewis A. Jones, were very helpful to my understanding of him both as a man and a scholar. I am also grateful to the dedicated librarians and archivists at the University of North Carolina, Atlanta University, Savannah State College, the University of Chicago, and the Department of Archives and History of North Carolina. Daniel T. Williams, the archivist at Tuskegee Institute, must be singled out for both his aid in locating pertinent materials in the various collections at the school and his generous personal support and assistance in many ways.

Like all writers, I am also indebted to the numerous scholars who preceded me. Few have written about Monroe Work, but many have studied issues and events pertinent to his career. Not all of the books and articles that were helpful to me are cited, but I have endeavored to note the more useful ones in the footnotes.

Finally, a number of individuals—including Allen W. Jones, Joseph P. Hobbs, John David Smith, Louis Harlan, James H. Jones, and Kenneth P. Vickery—have given aid and support in various forms. Elaine Jones and Annette Thomlinson deserve mention for their patience and good humor in the face of many alterations of the manuscript on the word processor. I am also grateful to Les Phillabaum, William Cooper, Beverly Jarrett, and Catherine Barton at Louisiana State University Press for their encouragement and help. No one contributed more than Richard M. McMurry, who provided expert professional advice and support beyond the call of duty for any spouse.

RECORDER OF THE
BLACK EXPERIENCE

Introduction / The Truth Shall Set Us Free

Racism is deeply rooted in the American past, and theories of black inferiority have been as abundant as the varieties of exploitation that they justified. Never, however, was prejudice as virulent and widely accepted as during the period referred to as the nadir of the black experience in the United States, when Monroe Nathan Work began his career as a sociologist. The years at the turn of the twentieth century witnessed a steady deterioration in race relations. The bright hopes raised by emancipation and Reconstruction rapidly faded in an increasingly hostile environment marked by lynchings, race riots, disfranchisement, and new Jim Crow laws. As Negrophobia became a southern obsession, most Americans turned their backs, and both political parties, as well as all three branches of the federal government, abdicated responsibility for the protection of blacks' rights.

The political desertion of blacks was a natural consequence of the rampant racism among the general public. The actions of politicians are usually accurate barometers of the public mood, and in the popular conception, blacks were pictured as less than human. One writer even declared that God had created the Negro as the highest form of beast "with articulate speech, and hands, that he may be of service to his master—the white man." He insisted that "under the law of God the Negro, like every other animal, is the property of man," and he traced almost all social ills to the notion, which he found absurd, that blacks were human.[1]

More frequently blacks were depicted in works written for the

1. Charles Carroll, *The Negro a Beast* (St. Louis, 1900), 1, 288.

general public as a "lesser race" with numerous undesirable attributes. The popular novelist Thomas Dixon, Jr., described the Negro as "a creature, with a racial record of four thousand years of incapacity, half-child, half-animal, the sport of impulse, whim and conceit, pleased with a rattle, tickled with a straw, a being who left to his own will, roams at night and sleeps in the day, whose native tongue has framed no word of love, whose passions once aroused are as a tiger."[2]

Even more discouraging to educated blacks was the growing acceptance of "scientific" racial doctrines that purported to prove the permanent inferiority of blacks and their incompatibility with white society. Various theories on the types of man emerged from the general movement to classify all living matter. In the nineteenth century the division of *Homo sapiens* into races was based on a multitude of physical criteria. Facial angles, bone structure, hair texture, skin color, and cranium size were all used to classify mankind. Most scholars agreed that race was a valid category; they simply could not agree on the number or origin of the races or on whether physical differences were accompanied by temperamental variations.

Some early writers advocated the theory of polygenesis, or the separate creation of the various races. For them, racial differences were much like species differences, and many argued that miscegenation produced biologically inferior "hybrids" with little or no reproductive abilities. Others could not break from the biblical tradition of common descent from Adam and Eve and thus attempted to explain physical differences in other ways. Most frequently they held that all men were originally Caucasian, but some had "degenerated" into the inferior races. Few questioned the natural superiority of the "European type," either physically or temperamentally. The emergence of Darwinian concepts of evolution dramatically altered the nature of the argument but not its impact on Afro-Americans. Although ideas such as natural selection helped explain the origin of differing gene pools, the theory of the survival

2. Thomas Dixon, Jr., "Booker T. Washington and the Negro," *Saturday Evening Post*, August, 19, 1905, pp. 1–2.

of the fittest gave new impetus to assertions of black inferiority. The political dominance of whites in the late nineteenth century provided proof to the social Darwinists that Caucasians were biologically superior. Indeed, some believed that blacks were destined to lose the struggle for survival in the United States and looked forward to a solution of the race problem through black attrition.[3] In an 1896 publication of the American Economic Association, Frederick L. Hoffman held that because of their unsuitability American Negroes were dying out and that educational, religious, and philanthropic efforts to help them had only increased their dependency and had not led to a "higher appreciation of the stern and uncompromising virtues of the Aryan race."[4]

The majority of white scholars in all fields accepted the basic premise of black inferiority. The combined writings of historians, anthropologists, sociologists, and psychologists gave apparently irrefutable evidence that Africans had never accomplished much and that their descendents could be expected to contribute even less. To most Americans, therefore, any achievement by Afro-Americans could only be explained by either the presence of "white blood" or the "imitative powers of the Negro." As one white southerner wrote, "I have seen the circus-horse Champion dance. He danced most infamously, but without a doubt his education had cost him ten thousand lashes; Negroes sometimes learn to read about as well as Champion danced, for their organs of speech are as unfitted for reading as the horse's legs for dancing."[5]

To educated blacks, the popular and scientific concepts of white supremacy were more than personal affronts. They realized that the widespread acceptance of these doctrines provided much of the ammunition for depriving blacks of their basic rights as Americans. When the question of higher education for blacks arose, the

---

3. See Peter I. Rose, *The Subject Is Race* (New York, 1968); George M. Fredrickson, *The Black Image in the White Mind* (New York, 1972); Michael Banton, *The Idea of Race* (Boulder, 1977); John S. Haller, Jr., *Outcasts from Evolution* (Urbana, 1971).

4. Frederick L. Hoffman, *Race Traits and Tendencies of the American Negro*, Publications of the American Economic Association, XI (New York, 1896), 329.

5. Quoted in Gilbert Osofsky, *The Burden of Race* (New York, 1968), 184–85.

answer was often similar to that of Dr. Charles S. Bacon: "A classical education for a negro whose proper vocation is raising rice or cotton or garden truck, is as much out of place as a piano in a Hottentot's tent."[6]

In a country where democratic principles were proclaimed, strong arguments were needed to justify the denial of basic political rights to one class of citizens. Racist theory provided the solution. Thus a discriminatory grandfather clause that allowed uneducated whites to vote but denied suffrage to blacks could be defended, even in the face of the Fifteenth Amendment, by a delegate to the Alabama Constitutional Convention of 1901.

> These provisions are justified in law and in morals, because it is said that the negro is not discriminated against on account of his race, but on account of his intellectual and moral condition. There is a difference it is claimed with great force, between the uneducated white man and the ignorant negro. There is in the white man an inherited capacity for government which is wholly wanting in the negro. Before the art of reading and writing was known, the ancestors of the Anglo-Saxon had established an orderly system of government, the basis, in fact, of the one under which we now live. That the negro, on the other hand, is descended from a race lowest in intelligence and moral perception of all the races of men.[7]

Similarly, whites argued that segregation was needed to preserve the purity and accomplishments of the superior white race from contamination by miscegenation. Southerners found many northern allies in this cause, including a professor at the University of Pennsylvania, who wrote that miscegenation "would be a shameful sacrifice, fraught with evil to the entire species. It is an unpardonable sale of a noble birthright for a mess of potage. We cannot cloud or extinguish the fine nervous susceptibility, and mental force, which cultivation develops in the constitution of the Indo-European, by the fleshy instincts, and dark mind of the African. . . . The greatest danger which flows from the presence of the negro in this country is the certainty of the contamination of the race."[8]

Perhaps nowhere was justice more perverted by racism than in

6. Haller, *Outcasts*, 59.
7. Quoted in Osofsky, *Burden of Race*, 175–76.
8. Quoted in Haller, *Outcasts*, 200.

the defense of lynching. This barbaric practice flourished at the turn of the century in part because both scholars and laymen believed blacks to have inherently different sexual instincts. Blacks, as beings lower on the evolutionary ladder, were said to be dominated by "animal passions." The literature of the day included lurid and titillating descriptions of black men eager to rape white women. "The black brute is lurking in the dark, a monstrous beast, crazed with lust. His ferocity is almost demonical. A mad bull or tiger could scarcely be more brutal," wrote one author in 1901.[9] Lynching was seen as a necessary evil to prevent an even greater one.

The idea of black inferiority was so pervasive that even those whites who sought to protect black rights were usually touched by it. Most racial liberals of the day did not deny white supremacy; they only expressed a paternalistic concern for the weak and defenseless Negro. Among white scholars, it was the sociologists who confronted the issue of race relations most directly. In general, however, they viewed blacks as a social problem and advocated that "the socially superior race [whites] should have good will and assist the socially inferior race on the other side of the fence."[10]

Black response to the epidemic of racism and the discrimination it produced was as diverse and confused as the black population itself. Some, engulfed in self-hate, sought to become white; others renounced all European culture and values. Most, however, worked in various ways through the prevailing channels of influence for redress of injustices, although white domination of such institutions as the press and the government led to disagreement over the best tactics to use to secure the basic rights of citizenship and humanity for Afro-Americans. By 1905 two main styles of leadership had evolved: those of the accommodationist Booker T. Washington and the activist W. E. B. Du Bois. Their basic disagreement was not whether blacks deserved the privileges afforded to whites but how these could be most effectively won in an age of violence and an atmosphere of white supremacy. Should blacks band together for self-help and solidarity, or should they seek alliances with the

9. Quoted in Fredrickson, *Black Image*, 278.
10. E. Franklin Frazier, "Sociological Theory and Race Relations," *American Sociological Review*, XII (June, 1947), 267.

white majority? Should they strive to make the best of the opportunities still available, or should they insist on the full rights of
manhood here and now? These were the unsettling questions that
shook the foundations of individual belief as well as the entire
structure of race leadership. Immediate methods, not ultimate
aims, separated Washington and Du Bois, but the fundamental issue was human dignity, and controversy over method aroused
deeply emotional responses.[11]

Black scholars were somewhat isolated from the worst barbari-
ties of racism, but they faced ideological and psychological dilemmas unperceived by the masses. As contradictions to the dominant
racial theories, they were considered as useful as pianos in the
tents of Hottentots and as exotic as dancing horses. Their minds
and their training naturally created the desire to be accepted as legitimate scholars while society refused to recognize them fully as
men. Some may have desired a status distinct from that of less educated blacks, but even the academic community would not allow
it. Such men were not historians, sociologists, or writers; they were
Negro historians, Negro sociologists, and Negro writers, whose
proper subject matter for research was "the Negro."[12]

Although circumstances may have prevented them from doing
otherwise, some chose black subjects out of a sense of black na-
tionalism. Others felt a keen responsibility. When white scholarship seemed determined to prove black inferiority, who but blacks
were left to refute the claim? Those who went to northern schools
and competed successfully with white students knew their example had an impact. At the very least their white colleagues had
to admit that they danced very well, for horses. To these blacks
their own success proved the errors of the prevailing racial theories. It seemed a simple matter: expose the falsehoods and the discrimination that they justified would cease. Then all blacks would

11. See August Meier, *Negro Thought in America, 1880–1915* (Ann Arbor,
1963); Louis R. Harlan, *Booker T. Washington: The Making of a Black Leader,
1856–1901* (New York, 1972); Elliott Rudwick, *W. E. B. Du Bois: Propagandist
of the Negro Protest* (New York, 1968).

12. John Hope Franklin, "The Dilemma of the American Negro Scholar," in
Herbert Hill (ed.), *Soon, One Morning: New Writing by American Negroes,
1940–1962* (New York, 1963), 60–76.

be accepted as human beings. As Monroe Work wrote in 1929, "In the end facts will help eradicate prejudice and misunderstanding, for facts are the truth and the truth shall set us free."[13]

Simple solutions proved elusive to the black scholar, however. Merely stating the truth did not guarantee its acceptance. The facts must reach the right audience and have the desired impact. Meanwhile, for the individual many questions remained. Should he remain aloof from the everyday problems of his fellow blacks, isolated in his "ivory tower," to prove his scientific detachment? Or should he use his talents more directly for the benefit of his people? Each man had to ask himself, Just what is the extent of my responsibility? These were not easy questions, and the "Talented Tenth," as Du Bois called them, responded in different ways to the dilemma of being both black and bright.

For numerous reasons Monroe Nathan Work is a perfect subject for a case study of this dilemma. Born of former slaves, he was a southerner who ventured North to receive an advanced degree from the University of Chicago and then returned to the South. His career followed a discursive path, which eventually led him to Tuskegee Institute, where he founded the Department of Records and Research in 1908. Caught in the middle of the Washington–Du Bois controversy, Work responded in a way that lends insight into the ideological quandary of the black intellectual. His faith in the potential of his people and his dream of eliminating prejudice through education reflect the driving force behind many of the black scholars of his day. Finally, his life reveals something of the frustrations, as well as the joys, of black intellectuals from the turn of the century until World War II, or for that matter, of any person with what seems at times an impossible dream.

13. Tuskegee *Messenger*, March 9, 1929.

I / You Can't Argue
with Facts

All people are shaped by the events and the temper of their age, as well as by the social groups to which they belong. This was especially true for blacks during Monroe Work's lifetime. No black, regardless of income or talent, could completely escape the dehumanizing reminders of the prejudice and discrimination that created what is called "the black experience." Nevertheless, every life is unique. Blacks also encountered the world as individuals; there were as many black experiences as there were blacks. They lived in the North, South, East, and West, in cities and in rural environments. Some lives seem to transcend the personal struggles and successes of a single individual, however, and reveal the human predicament of the entire group. Such was the life of Monroe Work.

Like all Americans at the turn of the century, he witnessed rapid social change. As a black, he experienced the new mobility growing from emancipation and lived in a variety of environments, pursuing diverse occupations, before becoming a member of the black intelligentsia. His experiences gave him a wider view of black life than many of his colleagues and help explain how he could move from participation in Du Bois' activist Niagara Movement to Washington's accommodationist Tuskegee Institute.

Unlike most pioneer black sociologists, Work was the son of former slaves and grew up in a rural environment. Born in Iredell County, North Carolina, on August 15, 1866, he did not personally experience slavery, but he had more than just an academic acquaintance with slave life. His mother, Eliza Hobbs, his father, Alexander Work, and eight of his brothers and sisters had been slaves. On the other hand, he also had some knowledge of the expe-

8

rience of antebellum free blacks, because his grandfather, Henry Work, had obtained his freedom and moved to Decatur, Michigan, where he became a brickmason.[1]

Henry Work's skill may have enabled him to purchase his freedom, for slave artisans and craftsmen were sometimes hired out by their masters and allowed to keep a portion of their earnings. To buy one's way out of bondage was always difficult and was technically illegal in antebellum North Carolina. Thus, Henry Work's accomplishment likely meant that he had a reasonable master and an ample supply of ability and determination. Before emancipation he had also purchased freedom for his wife and all but three of his children, one of whom was Monroe's father, Alexander.[2]

Monroe's parents were married on December 18, 1847, after Eliza's owners, the Poston family, had purchased Alexander for $1,400. The purchase may have been made to facilitate the marriage. Many owners had discovered that slave marriages were beneficial to plantation management. The slaves were more content, and family ties were a deterrent to running away. If slave marriages were good for the masters, they were doubly so for the slaves, providing one of the best mechanisms for maintaining a sense of individuality and self-worth. For that reason, slave marriages were remarkably stable and long lasting, especially considering such obstacles as the lack of legal recognition and the possibility of separation by sale. Certainly, the Works' marriage reflected that durability; it lasted forty-two years, ending only with the death of Eliza Work. Fortunately, their master was neither inclined nor forced by financial necessity to sell either of them.[3]

The Works were also fortunate in other ways. Their living conditions do not seem to have been as bleak as those of some slaves, and they had eight children during their eighteen years together as slaves. Three more, including Monroe, were born after emancipa-

1. Jessie P. Guzman, "Monroe Nathan Work and His Contributions," *Journal of Negro History*, XXXIV (October, 1949), 428.

2. *Ibid.*; John Hope Franklin, *The Free Negro in North Carolina, 1790–1860* (Chapel Hill, 1943).

3. Guzman, "Work," 428; see John W. Blassingame, *The Slave Community* (New York, 1972); Herbert G. Gutman, *The Black Family in Slavery and Freedom, 1750–1925* (New York, 1976).

tion. However, the limits to the bonds of affection between even a paternalistic master and his slaves are clearly indicated by both Poston's and the Works' response to emancipation. Alexander Work was eager to leave the plantation, and Poston did not try to detain him, giving him instead a "sack of spare ribs and backbone" and sending him into the world to find some means to support his family. That was hardly generous compensation for eighteen years of almost free labor.[4]

Like most freedmen in 1865, Alexander Work had little more than his freedom. He quickly decided to leave Iredell County and the South. To some extent he may have been following the example of his father, but there were probably numerous reasons for his departure. Other blacks were also leaving the county, largely because of the attitudes and practices of whites. While some whites bemoaned the loss of a cheap labor force, most rejected the idea of any true emancipation. A county newspaper declared in May, 1866, that Africans were "heathens, savages—eating each other for food, going quite naked and are as wild and cannibal as the animals that roam the forests and jungles." Former slaves should therefore "be thankful . . . that they were brought from Africa and . . . sold . . . as slaves to the Christian people of the South."[5]

Such attitudes were overtly expressed in Iredell County in a number of ways. Monthly wages for blacks in the area were only ten dollars for men and five dollars for women in 1866. Even these wages were not low enough to suit some whites, and blacks all over North Carolina were arrested for minor offenses and bound out as apprentices for nominal fees; six such cases occurred in Iredell County in 1866. In addition, there was opposition to educating blacks. A local minister noted that almost half the citizens of his town had refused to sign a document proposing that "the freedmen sh'ld have a school."[6]

Along with discrimination, blacks faced a problem also con-

4. Guzman, "Work," 428–29.

5. Robert Delmer Miller, *Of Freedom and Freedmen: Racial Attitudes of White Elites in North Carolina During Reconstruction, 1865–1877* (Ann Arbor, 1976), 58; Roberta Sue Alexander, *North Carolina Faces the Freedmen: Race Relations During Presidential Reconstruction, 1865–1867* (Ann Arbor, 1974), 113.

6. Alexander, *North Carolina Faces the Freedmen*, 483, 595, 606.

fronting their white neighbors—a severe drought that drastically lowered the agricultural production of the piedmont area in 1866. With such conditions, it is amazing that it only took about a year for Alexander Work to earn enough money to buy a wagon and mule team and leave Iredell County. Like his father, he went north, temporarily leaving his family behind, but instead of Decatur, Michigan, he chose Cairo, Illinois.[7]

The choice of Cairo is in some ways puzzling. Located at the confluence of the Ohio and Mississippi rivers, it was the southern terminus of the railroad in Illinois. Swampy conditions thwarted two attempts at settlement, in 1818 and 1837; and only in 1846, with the coming of the railroad, was a permanent settlement finally established. A levee was built by the Illinois Central railway, and by 1855 the town's population had reached a thousand. By the early 1860s Cairo was still far from a paradise; one traveler called it "a cheerless, miserable place, sacred to the ague and fever" and declared that it was "wonderful if the people can live on any food but quinine." A British visitor noted that "anything more dismal than the prospects from the window of the St. Charles Hotel, out of which I looked over the whole city, can hardly be conceived. The heat was as great as that of the hottest of the dog-days with us, and the air was laden with a sort of sultry vapor we scarcely know of in England." He went on to recount the popular version of the area's origins. "A Yankee legend states," he wrote, "that when the universe was allotted out between heaven, earth, and hell, there was one allotment intended for the third department, and crowded by mistake into the second; and to this topographical error Cairo owes its terrestrial existence."[8]

There were those who found the city appealing, however. It was the closest free-soil location, and it was farther south than Richmond, Virginia, or Lexington, Kentucky, and was well suited to such southern crops as tobacco, wheat, corn, and hemp. Both factors made the area attractive to white small-scale farmers, many of whom came to Cairo hoping to escape the presence of blacks. From

7. *Ibid.*, 466; Guzman, "Work," 429.
8. Paul M. Angle (ed.), *Prairie State: Impressions of Illinois, 1673–1967* (Chicago, 1969), 311–12, 335, 352.

the beginning, the area was noted for its Negrophobia. The city acquired a distinctly southern aura with "magnolias and bald cy-
presses" as well as "the soft speech of Dixie." To the dismay of the
whites, however, Cairo's location also made it a natural escape
route for fugitive slaves. The whites quickly returned as many es-
capees as they could and made it clear that blacks were not wel-
come. The Cairo *Gazette* even bragged that one fugitive had volun-
tarily surrendered, saying that "four days free in Cairo were worse
than four years in bondage."[9]

Nevertheless, after the war Cairo acquired a sizable population
of blacks, Monroe Work's father among them. He apparently fared
well in Cairo, for in about a year he earned enough money to send
for his family. He worked primarily as a tenant farmer but lived one
winter on the farm of a livestock dealer. The Works remained in
Cairo for nine years and Alexander's relative success created a
rather stable environment for Monroe's crucial childhood years. In
Cairo the boy acquired his first knowledge of the alphabet from a
Sunday school speller and obtained some formal schooling.[10]

Education and land were two of the most desired goals among the
freedmen. In Cairo, Monroe received some of the former, but his father was unable to acquire the latter. Thus, in the 1870s Alexander
Work followed the example of others and moved to Kansas, again
temporarily leaving his family behind. He was part of the first great
wave of black migration, which peaked in 1879 and increased Kansas' black population from about 16,250 in 1870 to 43,110 in 1880.
Most of these emigrants came from the former slave states where
conditions had steadily deteriorated after the end of Reconstruction in 1876–1877. They were fleeing the same kind of economic
exploitation, political repression, educational handicaps, and social
humiliation that the Works had tried to escape ten years earlier and
that had only grown worse over the years.

9. Eugene H. Berwanger, *The Frontier Against Slavery* (Urbana, 1971), 8;
Angle (ed.), *Prairie State*, 570; V. Jacque Voeglei, *Free but Not Equal: The Mid-
west and the Negro During the Civil War* (Chicago, 1967), 8–9.
10. Guzman, "Work," 429; Monroe N. Work, "Education and the Negro"
(Typescript, n.d., in Box 3, Monroe Nathan Work Papers, Tuskegee Institute
Archives).

The exodusters were also drawn to Kansas for positive reasons. Like Work, they wanted to live in a free-soil state, and Kansas was described as the "home of John Brown" by emigrationists such as Moses "Pap" Singleton and Henry Adams. Work had already learned that prejudice did not stop at the Mason-Dixon Line and that free-soilism was rooted more in a desire to keep the West a "white man's country" than in an abolitionist antagonism to the inhumanity of slavery. In fact, prior to the war many of the free-soil states had debated—and several had adopted—black exclusion laws or other discriminatory legislation. During Reconstruction many such laws were repealed, however, and blacks believed there was more freedom and better opportunity for them in Kansas than in the South.[11]

The flood of black emigrants often created cracks in the thin crust of Kansas tolerance, and both black and white settlers discovered that much of the state was hardly a garden of Eden. But the most powerful magnet of all was land and many settlers, including Alexander Work, succeeded in acquiring it. Their success can be largely accounted for by two pieces of legislation: the Preemption Act and the Homestead Act. The first allowed a settler who lived on and improved federal land for at least six months to purchase 160 acres at $1.25 per acre after it was surveyed and put on public sale. The Homestead Act made it possible for a person to stake a claim to 160 acres at a federal land office and to acquire the land for a nominal filing fee after five years of residence. The provisions of both acts aided land speculators more than small farmers, but they did enable Alexander Work and thousands of others to become independent farmers.

Work preempted a 160-acre farm in Sumner County, near Aston, ten miles west of Arkansas City and not far from the Indian Territory. It was the sod-house frontier. The lack of trees on the Kansas plains necessitated some innovative approaches, and Work, like the other settlers, built a house made of bricks cut from the thick, strong sod found in the low spots on the prairie. He also enclosed

11. Guzman, "Work," 429; see Nell Irvin Painter, *Exodusters: Black Migration to Kansas After Reconstruction* (New York, 1976).

the entire homestead with a hedge that substituted for wood fencing, unavailable on the prairie.

His family soon joined him, and they divided the homestead into three plots—eighty acres for cultivation, forty for hay, and forty for pasture. The major crops were wheat, corn, and oats. Apparently they were fairly successful for they remained there thirteen years, and Monroe completed his elementary education at a nearby school located in a church, which served as a center for all community activities.[12]

Gradually, Monroe's brothers and sisters married and left the farm, until only one brother remained to help him run the farm and care for their aging, invalid parents. The entire responsibility eventually fell to Monroe, and although he deeply desired to continue his education, he stayed on the farm until his mother died in 1889 and his father went to live with one of the married children. Only then, at age twenty-three, did he pursue his dream of more education.[13]

Those twenty-three years had not been wasted. Work had learned a lot about patience, responsibility, and the plight of the black farmer. He would never feel the remoteness from the problems of common folk that characterized a segment of the black bourgeoisie. Having lived in only two places that he could remember, he had also probably acquired a sense of stability that sustained him during the next ten years as he struggled to find his place in life.

Free at last to seek his own destiny, Work soon encountered the obstacles and detours that often plague such a quest. Some of his indecision and problems were typical of most young people, others were characteristic only of black youth, and some were unique. When he enrolled in high school in Arkansas City, his major problems were supporting himself and being older than most of his classmates. Much of his energy went into meeting the first challenge; he worked at a variety of odd jobs, including assisting in a surgical operation.

Soon the strain seemed to be too much, and Work decided that he was too old to be in school. Filled with discouragement, he made

12. Guzman, "Work," 429.
13. *Ibid.*, 429–30.

his way to the superintendent's office to inform him of his decision to leave school. Fortunately, the superintendent, David Ross Boyd, who later became the first president of the University of Oklahoma, found the right words to inspire Work with a new sense of hope and dedication.[14]

Boyd's time and effort were well spent; Work became an outstanding student by the time of his graduation in June, 1892. Boyd ranked him as the best mathematician in the school's history and wrote a glowing letter of recommendation: "He is a young man of most excellent character, studious and careful. He has shown an untiring spirit in the effort to procure an education, standing third in his class. I heartily recommend him to any Board desiring an able, trustworthy teacher of thorough scholarship and good Christian character."[15]

By that time Work had acquired more confidence. He wanted to continue his education but knew he needed money to reach that goal. He soon learned that there were few opportunities for educated blacks other than teaching or preaching. Deciding to teach, he quickly discovered that although integrated school systems provided increased opportunities for black students, they offered few for black teachers. Even with his record and Boyd's letter of recommendation, he was unable to find a teaching position in Arkansas City. Blacks were sometimes allowed to teach Indians, and Work therefore sought a job among the Creek and Cherokee in the Indian Territory. Again he was unsuccessful, but he was finally hired by a private school. It was not an inspiring experience; for his efforts he received only "room and board and malaria."[16]

As Boyd's letter testified, Work was a very religious person and soon turned to the other area open to educated blacks. He was ordained as a minister in the African Methodist Episcopal church, the denomination founded in 1794 by Richard Allen in reaction against the prejudice encountered in white churches. The AME church, first established in Philadelphia, spread rapidly in the North before the war and in the South after it, its success reflecting the desire of blacks to control their religious life. Work assumed a

14. *Ibid.*, 430.
15. Letter of recommendation, June 22, 1892, as cited *ibid.*
16. Guzman, "Work," 431.

pastorate in Wellington, Kansas, in late 1892, but he remained only a few months. Blacks often established their own churches not only to escape white prejudice but to engage in a more emotional form of worship. This desire was even more pronounced in rural, frontier churches in places like Wellington. Work, however, was hardly dynamic or charismatic. His demeanor, even then, was decidedly scholastic, and his lips barely moved when he talked. His congregation quickly decided that it wanted another man.[17]

By this time Work was discouraged. His attempts to use his education to acquire the funds for more schooling had failed utterly. Naturally he returned to the occupation at which he had been successful—farming. In September, 1893, the federal government opened the Cherokee Outlet in Oklahoma to settlement, and Work decided to stake a claim.

Typically, when any new area was opened, hordes of aspiring settlers began congregating on the border days ahead of time and had to be restrained by soldiers posted along the boundary line. In 1893 desperation, rather than hope, was the dominant emotion. To victims of the drought of 1892–1893 on the Great Plains, this land represented a last chance, for the public domain was rapidly vanishing. Tension was also increased by blistering hundred-degree heat and swirling dust; there had been no rain since July and water was being sold at a premium. Violence was common as the masses of would-be settlers in all kinds of transportation awaited the round of gunshots that would signal the beginning of the race for the best land. After the race finally began, Work's party of six led the others at the end of three miles. All managed to stake their claims, and Work spent the night on the lot of a friend in nearby Perry, Oklahoma.[18]

Others were not as lucky. One potential settler was found with his throat slit, and at least one black was driven from a claim by the threat of lynching and cries of "That's right, we don't want any niggers in this country." Work's triumph was somewhat diminished

17. John Hope Franklin, *From Slavery to Freedom* (4th ed.; New York, 1974), 117; Guzman, "Work," 431.

18. H. Wayne Morgan and Anne Hodges, *Oklahoma* (New York, 1977), 55; Florence Work, interview, as cited in Guzman, "Work," 431–32.

when the land office opened the next morning and he discovered that another person had staked the same claim. Fortunately, the dispute was settled peacefully by dividing the 160 acres equally between the two claimants. Work moved onto his 80-acre plot in March, 1894, living in an eight-by-twelve-foot tool shed he had bought for twenty dollars. That year he planted twenty-five acres in wheat and the following year, thirteen acres of flax.[19]

Work's dream of resuming his education was once again deferred—this time by a long illness and a slow recovery. Once he was fit again, he took a job delivering cattle to the meat packing companies in Chicago, "going up on a caboose and returning on a pass." The job supplemented the income from the farm, which was never sufficient to provide extra funds for his education. In the winter of 1895 he took a test for a teaching position in Kay County. His ability in mathematics made him the only person able to solve all the math questions on the examination, and he won the highest mark on the test, but had to settle for the salary accorded holders of a second-grade certificate. His score apparently could not bleach the color of his skin in the eyes of the school board members, who announced that they were not bound by the results of an examination they had not given. Work learned a valuable lesson that was reflected later in his many studies of the pay differential between black and white teachers.[20]

His frustrating experience with the school board and his exposure to Chicago through the cattle job renewed his resolve to seek more education. He had decided to return to the ministry and probably realized that he would need advanced training to qualify for the sort of pastorate in which intellectualism rather than emotionalism was expected from the minister. He therefore entered the Chicago Theological Seminary, but his three years there produced a sociologist—not a minister. "I realized," he later wrote, "that a theological education was not a very good education being too limited in extent."[21]

19. Morgan and Hodges, *Oklahoma*, 55; Guzman, "Work," 432; Perry Cash Certificate #65, in Record Group 49, National Archives.

20. Guzman, "Work," 432.

21. Monroe Work to Florence Hendrickson, August 4, 1904, as cited *ibid*.

His mathematical skills and interests made sociology attractive to him, and his choice of theology schools aided his discovery of that profession. As the leading Congregational school in the Middle West, the Chicago Theological Seminary was in the forefront of the social gospel movement, which sought "to reorient the historic faith of America to an industrial society" and to kindle reformist zeal to tackle the ills of that society. Social problems had to be highlighted and studied before churches could seek solutions. Thus, in 1892 the Chicago Seminary established the first department of Christian sociology and chose William Graham Taylor as its chairman.[22]

After insisting upon "unrestricted liberty" to "study, teach, and exemplify the application of our common Christianity to . . . social conditions," Taylor accepted the position largely because of the challenges of the city of Chicago. There was no better place to test the power of the social gospel than in the slums of that sprawling industrial center. In his inaugural address he promised to teach students "to observe social and industrial conditions, classify facts, and draw conclusions for themselves." Always stressing the importance of field work, he established the Chicago Commons, a settlement house, in 1894 so that he could teach Christian sociology "from the ground up and not from the clouds down." He taught his students about the importance of group relationships and the impact of society upon the individual. "The channel through which life is now sweeping is less individualistic than sociological in its formation," he wrote. "All human life and interests, industrial and political, intellectual and spiritual . . . contribute toward the pull of this social gravity. Apart from these influences, not only is society not to be understood, but the individual may not be intelligently treated." It was the duty of Christian sociology, he asserted, "to investigate the conditions of social and personal life, discover the causes of suffering and the sources of inharmonious relations." Only then would it be possible "to adjust the deficiencies, and harmonize the varying elements."[23]

22. Charles Howard Hopkins, *The Rise of the Social Gospel in American Protestantism* (New Haven, 1940), 12; Louis C. Wade, *Graham Taylor: Pioneer for Social Justice, 1851–1930* (Chicago, 1964), 47.

23. Wade, *Graham Taylor*, 48, 95, 81, 42, 45–46.

Taylor was noted for drawing on his students' backgrounds and interests in his classroom, and so, black problems became one focus of his Christian sociology course after Work enrolled in 1897. With Taylor's guidance and encouragement, the young man embarked on a "study of Negro crime in Chicago as sort of a term paper." Work's talent for research was quickly revealed, as was the influence of his teacher on his thinking. The paper stressed the correlation between poverty and crime, showing statistically that the highest crime rates occurred in the slums of the city. The higher crime rates for blacks could thus be explained by the large proportion of them living in slums. The settlement house movement, which provided aid and guidance to slum dwellers, had helped alleviate the problems in some areas. But, Work noted, blacks had generally been ignored in this movement.[24]

Three years later the paper, with some revisions, became the first article written by a black to be published in the *American Journal of Sociology*. At that time the practical value of exposing social problems through solid research was dramatically illustrated for Work. A businessman in Sacramento, California, was so disturbed by the implications of the article that he wrote Jane Addams of Hull House offering a hundred dollars as seed money for a fund to establish settlement houses for blacks in Chicago.[25]

By that time Work had crossed the bridge to sociology, enrolling in the sociology department at the University of Chicago in 1898. Taylor had provided the bridge, but the journey was not a long one, either mentally or physically. There were close links between the seminary and the university. Taylor had been asked to join the faculty at the university in 1896 and later served as part-time lecturer from 1903 to 1906. Moreover, the sociology department was closely tied to the divinity school at the University of Chicago. The first two members of the department were originally trained as ministers, and the whole university was founded as a Baptist institution in 1891 through an endowment by John D. Rockefeller. Like Tay-

24. *Ibid.*, 98, 99; Monroe N. Work, interview by Lewis A. Jones, May 15, 1932 (Transcript in Box 1, Jessie P. Guzman Papers, Tuskegee Institute Archives), hereinafter cited as Jones interview.
25. Monroe N. Work, "Crime Among the Negroes of Chicago," *American Journal of Sociology*, VI (September, 1900), 204–23; Guzman, "Work," 435.

(Right) Monroe Work as a student in Chicago

(Below) Work in his room in Divinity Hall at the University of Chicago

lor's Department of Christian Sociology, the university was service oriented. The education Work received there reinforced the lessons Taylor had taught. Throughout his life, Work would never be content merely to study social problems; he would actively crusade to solve them. Years later he spoke of the role of sociology: "If sociology has primarily to do with human beings in their associative capacities, then its primary function is thorough investigation and research, to collect a body of information that will point out, make clear, what these relationships are and what in the present, the now, should be done in order that these relationships may be made more harmonious, more just and proper."[26] For Work, sociology always remained a tool for changing social conditions.

His years at the University of Chicago did not eliminate the social gospel nature of his goals, but they did bring Work into the mainstream of the developing field of sociology. Like many of the social sciences, sociology was just beginning to be established on a professional basis in the 1890s. In fact, the department at Chicago, started in 1892, was the first separate department of sociology in the nation. The Chicago department continued to lead the field through its founder, Albion Small, who coauthored the first sociology textbook in 1894, founded the *American Journal of Sociology* in 1895, and cofounded the American Sociological Society ten years later. As a Baptist minister with a Ph.D. in history from Johns Hopkins, Small did not reject the meliorism of his chosen discipline but sought to give it respectability by insisting on scrupulous dedication to the facts. He believed that sociological findings should spur action—action based on knowledge, however, not emotion.[27]

In some ways, Work's metamorphosis into a sociologist paralleled the emergence of the discipline itself. He was in the right place at the right time and thus became one of the first black sociologists, sharing that honor with W. E. B. Du Bois, Kelly Miller, and Richard Wright, Jr. Like their white counterparts, all of these

26. Monroe N. Work, "Sociology in the Common Schools," *Proceedings of the American Sociological Society*, XIII (December, 1918), 95–97.

27. Fred H. Matthews, *Quest for an American Sociology: Robert E. Park and the Chicago School* (Montreal, 1977), 88–96.

pioneers began in different fields: Du Bois in history, Miller in mathematics, and Wright and Work in theology. At the beginning of any new discipline this is necessarily the case, and the work of the early sociologists reflected this convergence of fields. Thus, Work's career was representative, blending the spheres of sociology, history, and social welfare.

The dominance of Chicago in sociology is also indicated by the fact that two of the first four black sociologists began their training there. Monroe Work and Richard Wright, Jr., both entered in the summer of 1898. During that session there were about thirty blacks among some twenty-five hundred students. Most, including John Hope from Atlanta University, were teachers who only attended in the summer. When the fall term began, the black student population dropped to four, making Wright and Work half of the total group. The only other blacks on campus were two janitors.[28]

Despite differences in their backgrounds and studies, Wright and Work shared many common interests and quickly became friends. Wright was then in the divinity school but later received a Ph.D. in sociology from the University of Pennsylvania and eventually became a bishop in the African Methodist Episcopal church. His father was the president of the state college for blacks in Savannah, Georgia. Although Work's background was less privileged, he and the other black students became members of the black elite in Chicago. As Wright later noted, "Among the colored population a student at the university had a high social rating, and I was frequently invited to the homes of many colored people in the upper intellectual and economic brackets."[29] Undoubtedly the same was true for Work, and through such encounters his optimism regarding the potential and future of his people was very likely enhanced.

Work's faith in the power of education to eradicate prejudice was probably also boosted by the environment at the University of Chicago. Although such places were not immune to racism, the token blacks at northern white colleges clearly experienced less overt discrimination than most blacks. Wright marveled at the apparent

28. Jones interview; Richard R. Wright, Jr., *Eighty-seven Years Behind the Black Curtain* (Philadelphia, 1965), 40–41.
29. Wright, *Eighty-seven Years*, 67.

ease with which sacred southern racial taboos were broken: a white janitor insisted that Wright call him by his first name; a Princeton graduate in his New Testament class asked for his help with Greek; he was invited to meals in the homes of his professors.[30]

The four black students may have reveled in their new-found social status, but they also found that there were new responsibilities attached to it. They were expected to provide educational services for the blacks of the community. Work later recalled their efforts: "Richard Wright, junior, was at Chicago then and a fellow named Carney and a fellow named Young. We were the only colored students at the University. We would go around to the churches, Wright would read a little Hebrew, I would read a little French, Carney some German, and Young some Greek." One of their educational efforts taught Work a valuable lesson. "We formed two debating teams: Wright and myself against Carney and Young. I learned the importance of facts. Wright and I had the facts and we would always get the decision because the other fellows might say the facts we offered weren't so but they couldn't offer any against them. You can't argue with facts."[31]

Work's contacts with black social leaders led him to attend the meetings of the Men's Sunday Club at a local church. At these meetings all sorts of literary and political topics were discussed. The programs varied, but many dealt with issues affecting blacks. By the time Work left Chicago in 1903, one of the paramount issues being talked about was the influence of Booker T. Washington. Catapulted to fame by his 1895 address at the Cotton States Exposition in Atlanta, the Tuskegean asserted that blacks should make the best of existing conditions in the South. His accommodationist program advocated temporarily subordinating agitation for political and civil rights to the quest for economic and educational advancement. Organized resistance to his ideas did not arise until 1905, but there were rumblings of discontent earlier, and apparently the Sunday Club split over Washington's approach to race problems. Work was in the anti-Washington faction.[32]

30. *Ibid.*, 39.
31. Jones interview.
32. C. E. Bentley to Work, April 25, 1905, in Box 2, Work Papers.

His acceptance by the black upper crust did not change the fact that Work was not wealthy and had to support himself while in school. To meet expenses, he held a number of jobs, including waiting on tables, doing janitorial work, and acting as campus agent for a city laundry service. In the latter position Work encountered another man who influenced the course of his career. After about a year in the sociology department, during which time he studied chiefly historical courses, Work delivered some laundry to William I. Thomas.[33]

Thomas was an outstanding figure in the early history of the University of Chicago's Department of Sociology. Born in 1863 in Tennessee, he was graduated from the University of Tennessee in 1884, taught there four years, studied philosophy in Germany for a year, and in 1889 was hired to teach English at Oberlin College. Because of his interest in "folk psychology"—or the study of the group mind through language, myth, and custom—he began to teach sociology at Oberlin and in 1895 became a fellow at Chicago, receiving one of the first doctorates there in 1896.[34]

It was Thomas' interest in folk psychology and social origins that first attracted Work to him, for this area of investigation seemed particularly appropriate to understanding the Afro-American culture. The young man was probably also impressed by the fact that Thomas did not accept the current theories of racial inferiority and had leveled particularly devastating blows at studies of cranial capacity and the inferences drawn from them. In fact, Thomas charged that "the classification of races has itself thus far proven an *ignis fatuus.*"[35]

Although Thomas rejected the usefulness of biological classifications of human beings, he did believe in the importance of social groupings and "the formation of artificial or historic races, through the influence of *milieu* and the diffusion of a common fund of beliefs, sentiments, ideas and interests among a heterogeneous population brought by hap and chance into the same geo-

33. Guzman, "Work," 435; Jones interview.
34. Matthews, *Quest for an American Sociology*, 97.
35. William I. Thomas, "The Scope and Method of Folk-Psychology," *American Journal of Sociology*, I (January, 1896), 434–45.

Work riding the bicycle he used to deliver laundry on campus, 1899

graphical zone." Because the individuals within such groups were profoundly influenced by their shared assumptions and values, an understanding of the "group mind," or folk psychology, was essential for interpreting the responses of the members, according to Thomas.[36]

He also asserted that while some temperamental differences might be biologically based, the development of the group mind of all peoples followed "similar and universal laws of growth." "Every community," he said, "as far as it rises toward a culture condition,

36. *Ibid.*

seems to take the same steps as every other community rising to the same level of culture." Thus, there are parallelisms in the growth patterns that are "manifestations of the practical identity of the human spirit." One constant, Thomas wrote, is that "every culture community contains in itself survivals of the earlier stages through which it has passed." Therefore, the social origins of a group are major keys to understanding its present condition.[37]

These ideas appealed to Monroe Work, and he began taking as much course work as possible from Thomas. The professor's intellectual influence can clearly be seen in the focus of Work's interest at that time. He perceived that "what Thomas was doing with social origins had connection with the study of the Negro" and so became much more interested in African culture and history. He began working in African materials and wrote a number of papers that were later published in the *Southern Workman*. Significantly, one series of these articles, entitled "Some Parallelisms in the Development of Africans and Other Races," compared the African solutions to human needs with those of other peoples.[38]

Work was also influenced by Thomas' ideas on the nature of prejudice. Thomas believed that prejudice originated in an instinctive fear of the different and unknown, which dated back to "the tribal stage of society when solidarity in feeling and action were essential to the preservation of the group." Through "reflex rather than deliberative experience," people perceive that the "outside world is antagonistic and subject to depredation" and respond with distrust to people who are physically different. "This prejudice is intense and immediate," Thomas wrote, "sharing in this respect the character of the instinctive reactions in general." However, "for all its intensity, race prejudice . . . is easily dissipated or converted into its opposite by association or a slight modification of stimulus." This was true, Thomas asserted, only if caste feeling did not intervene, making the "signs of superiority and inferiority" aids to "the manipulation of one class by another." Thomas believed that prejudice rooted in caste systems and arising out of "competitive

37. *Ibid.*
38. Jones interview.

activities" is difficult to overcome. Such prejudice would never completely disappear because a unity of "standards, tradition, and physical appearance in all geographical zones is neither possible nor aesthetically desirable," and prejudice can "neither be reasoned with nor legislated about very effectively." Diminishing the effects of race prejudice was not, however, a hopeless endeavor; Thomas asserted that prejudice "tends to become more insignificant as increased communication brings interests and standards in common, and as similar systems of education and equal access to knowledge bring about a greater mental and social parity between groups, and remove the grounds for 'invidious distinction.'"[39]

Some of the seeds of Work's response to racism are clearly seen in his mentor's words. He accepted wholeheartedly the idea that increased education of both whites and blacks was essential for improving relations between them. His own experiences with the "impact of fact" were thus reinforced. Thomas' emphasis on the need to bring about "a greater mental and social parity between groups" and on the futility of legislation against prejudice were perhaps among the factors that led Work to accept Booker T. Washington's program in 1908. After all, the keystone of Washington's accommodationism was that education and economic advancement could provide the only permanent foundation for political and civil rights for blacks. First, however, Work's path to Tuskegee was diverted by the influence of another man—W. E. B. Du Bois.

By the time Work left Chicago, Du Bois was already established as one of the foremost black intellectuals. During Work's sojourn at the university, Du Bois, recipient of the first Harvard Ph.D. granted to a black, published *The Suppression of the African Slave Trade to the United States of America, 1630–1870* and *The Philadelphia Negro*, became a professor at Atlanta University, and assumed the editorship of the Atlanta University Publications. It was in the latter role that Du Bois's relationship with Work developed. The Publications were the annual products of yearlong studies that focused on various aspects of black life. Numerous scholars were enlisted

39. William I. Thomas, "The Psychology of Race Prejudice," *American Journal of Sociology*, IX (March, 1904), 593–611.

in the effort and the results were presented at annual conferences and published. The eighteen monographs thus produced have been called "the first attempts to study scientifically the problems of the American Negro anywhere in the world; the first studies to make factual, empirical evidence the center of sociological work on the Negro."[40]

Work became involved in the Atlanta Studies while still a student in Chicago. The Atlanta Conference of 1903 was directed to the examination of the Negro church, and studies were made in various geographical areas of the current conditions of the churches and how they had changed during the preceding thirteen years. Work and Du Bois coauthored a study of black churches in Illinois and concluded that, although there had been improvement in the clergy, there was still a deplorable scarcity of college- and seminary-trained ministers. This condition, Work and Du Bois declared, prevented a large number of churches from meeting black intellectual needs and resulted in their declining appeal to young people. This joint assertion of the value of higher education foreshadowed the future link between the two men.[41]

The program at Atlanta appealed to Work because his own studies had been leading him in the same direction. His growing faith in the reformist power of sociology was displayed in a speech he delivered at a banquet during his student days. Entitled "The Importance of Sociology to the Negro," its thesis was that sociological research could provide a great service to blacks through the compilation of factual data, since no group had suffered more from a lack of knowledge concerning themselves. Years later, he spoke of his discovery. "It was then," he said, "that I dedicated my life to the gathering of information, the compiling of exact knowledge concerning the Negro."[42] Indeed, he had already started a collection of material on the Negro in "plain correspondence size envelopes"

40. Ernest Kaiser, Introduction to *Atlanta University Publications, Nos. 1, 2, 4, 8, 9, 11, 13, 14, 15, 16, 17, 18* (rpr. New York, 1968), iv.

41. W. E. B. Du Bois (ed.), *The Negro Church*, Atlanta University Publications, No. 8 (Atlanta, 1903), 83–92.

42. Monroe N. Work, Acceptance Speech for the Harmon Award, February 12, 1929 (Typescript in Box 1, Work Papers); Jones interview.

and "small notebooks" that later expanded to fill some thirty filing cabinets at Tuskegee Institute.

Completing his undergraduate studies in 1902, Work entered the University of Chicago's graduate program in sociology. His research centered around the subject that became his master's thesis: "The Negro Real Estate Owners of Chicago." He endeavored "to ascertain the number of Negroes owning property, the location and value of their holdings, the reasons for investing in real estate, and the relation of property owning to income, rent and segregation." Employing both historical and sociological methods, as in a large number of his articles, he traced black real estate holding back to Baptist Point de Saille, a Santo Domingan Indian trader who, Work asserted, had been the first property owner in Chicago in 1790. Work drew heavily on manuscript collections and census figures, but since county records did not give information on the race of real estate owners, he made a personal canvass of the city's blacks. Maps were interspersed throughout the paper to show the evolution of black real estate holdings. These maps illustrated by wards the total black population, the number of real estate owners, and the value and location of their holdings. In his conclusions Work implicitly indicated the far-reaching effects of residential segregation. Work noted that Negroes paid from 10 to 50 percent more per month for the same class of property as whites, and he drew the following picture of black conditions in Chicago:

> With new avenues of industry opening to the Negroes of Chicago and a fair amount of work resulting from the general prosperity of the city, the most pressing problem that confronts [the Negro] appears to be the Housing Problem. With a Negro population that is more than doubling itself each decade, the districts in the city in which he can live remain practically the same. This [leads to] overcrowded unsanitary districts, to high rents, the crowding of families into from two to four rooms, and the almost universal lodging system with its bad moral influence, the massing of the lewd and vicious with the respectable elements of the population, and its consequent tendencies to increase the crime rate.[43]

43. Monroe N. Work, "The Negro Real Estate Owners of Chicago" (M.A. thesis, University of Chicago, 1903).

The thesis drew praise from the press and from one of Work's teachers. Graham Taylor described the young scholar as "ever loyal to his race. . . . He began at the beginning in looking about him here in Chicago to find out what the actual conditions of his people were."[44]

His interest in discovering how blacks actually lived probably helped Work decide to go south after he received his Master of Arts degree on June 16, 1903. He had no need to search for a job upon graduation, for he had his choice of two positions. David Ross Boyd, the superintendent who had persuaded Work to remain in high school, wanted to create a place for him at Langston University in Oklahoma with the understanding that Work would move up to the presidency upon the retirement of Inman E. Page. His classmate, Richard Wright, Jr., had also persuaded his father, the president of Georgia State Industrial College in Savannah, to offer Work a job teaching education and history. After visiting both schools, Work decided to accept the potentially less lucrative position in Savannah, where more blacks were located. No doubt he was motivated by the same sense of racial responsibility that drew other members of the Talented Tenth to the Deep South.[45]

Perhaps another factor in his decision was the interest of Richard R. Wright, Sr., in studies of blacks. As an alumnus and trustee of Atlanta University, Wright had been a prime mover in establishing the Atlanta Studies. Also, the location at Savannah would put Work in close touch with Du Bois and his historic research project. Ironically, however, Work's return to the South ultimately led to his break with Du Bois. His life in Savannah would expose him to a different set of realities about the black experience. He had witnessed sporadic discrimination before, but he was about to become enmeshed in an environment of systematic repression in the land of white supremacy.

---

44. Chicago *Tribune*, June 17, 1903; Tuskegee *Student*, September 21, 1912; University of Chicago Convocation Program, June 16, 1903, in Box 1, Work Papers.

45. Guzman, "Work," 433.

II / Come from Their Closets of Seclusion

Savannah, where Monroe Work moved in 1903, was in some respects atypical of the South in its race relations. Like many port cities, it had both a large black population and an unusual degree of cosmopolitanism. When Work arrived, there were no city laws requiring segregation, and there was a real, if occasionally strained, spirit of cooperation between the white leaders and the black community. Conditions were far from ideal, but the history of race relations in Savannah offered some degree of hope for black advancement. Work apparently had an ideal laboratory in which to test the effectiveness of the tools for social improvement espoused by his mentors in Chicago. Yet within three years his optimism received a severe blow.

The cities of the South had always provided southern blacks with their best chance to establish viable communities and attain a relative degree of independence. Although the process was generally viewed with dismay by antebellum whites, urban slaves and freedmen were able to create and maintain black institutions and social networks. Savannah's free blacks, although not as prosperous as those of New Orleans or as progressive as those of Charleston, had succeeded in laying a foundation for freedom in the face of numerous legal and social barriers to economic advancement. By law they were excluded from some occupations and forced to purchase licenses not required of whites for others, but the laws were rarely enforced. By 1860 quite a few of the city's 705 free blacks had opened businesses and acquired property. Some even owned slaves. They had also led in the formation of quasi schools and five black churches and provided leadership to the black population, which

31

included many slaves who were skilled artisans or who had acquired business experience in other ways.

Black Savannahians had laid the foundation, but General William T. Sherman's arrival in 1864 created the conditions for building a true black community. Lured by army rations and the attrac-
tions of city life, thousands of newly liberated slaves converged on
the city, raising the total black population from 8,417 in 1860 to
13,068 in 1870. This black influx strained the relatively cordial race
relations and helped to increase the number of urban poor; it also
provided sufficient numbers for the establishment of black institutions and a rich social life.

The emerging black community created a native leadership
group that commanded some respect from the white establishment
and was able to take advantage of the political clout of the newly
enfranchised blacks. Using political pressure and the knowledge
that more blacks than whites were paying taxes for schools, they
were able to win support for black public schools in the 1870s. In
addition, they were able to prevent all attempts at enacting legal
segregation on the streetcars through black boycotts and the support of upper-class whites.[1]

The willingness of whites to compromise and a wide variety of
interracial contacts fostered by a relatively integrated housing pattern created an amazing degree of racial harmony, noted by both
blacks and whites, who were particularly proud that Savannah had
been immune to the virulent lynching spirit. The harmony was one
reason Savannah was selected as the site of the state college for
blacks.

In 1861 the United States Congress had given public lands to the
states to provide funds for the operation of agricultural and me-
chanical colleges. The precise use of the money received from the
Morrill Land-Grant Act was left to the discretion of the states. In

---

1. See Whittington B. Johnson, "Free Blacks in Antebellum Savannah: An
Economic Profile," *Georgia Historical Quarterly*, LXIV (Winter, 1980), 418–31;
John W. Blassingame, "Before the Ghetto: The Making of the Black Community
in Savannah, Georgia, 1865–1880," *Journal of Social History*, VI (Summer,
1973), 463–88; Robert E. Perdue, *The Negro in Savannah, 1865–1900* (New
York, 1973).

most southern states, of course, all the funds went to white colleges. By 1890 this situation troubled some northern consciences. Thus, when a second Morrill act increased the federal funding, a provision was tacked onto the bill requiring that some of the money go to southern blacks. Instead of admitting blacks to the white land-grant colleges, Georgia and the other southern states either assigned the revenue to established black schools or opened separate land-grant institutions. Georgia had contributed eight thousand dollars a year to Atlanta University until it was revealed that the school had a few white students. The idea of whites attending a black college disturbed the Georgia legislators, and in 1891 they opened a new land-grant school, Georgia State Industrial College, in Savannah and chose R. R. Wright, Sr., as president.[2]

One of the main reasons for establishing the school was the perceived need to control whatever institution received state funds. Consequently, a board of managers composed of white commissioners was created. They used their influence to see that some of their former servants were appointed to the industrial department, and they discouraged any course work resembling "higher education." R. R. Wright, Jr., later remembered and paraphrased the commencement speeches by the white commission chairman: "I believe in education for you people. The state of Georgia needs intelligent Negroes (pronounced 'Niggras'); but I do not believe in educating you people to want things you can never get. We must educate the Negro to be the best possible Negro and not a bad imitation of a white man."[3] These sentiments were shared by other commissioners, and in the 1890s they decided that no Greek, Latin, or higher mathematics should be taught. The students were infuriated by the restriction, and the academic professors, nearly all of whom were graduates of Atlanta University, promptly agreed to conduct the forbidden classes at night.[4]

R. R. Wright, Sr., was a skilled negotiator and administrator, and by the time Monroe Work arrived in 1903 the quality of the indus-

2. Richard R. Wright, Jr., *Eighty-seven Years Behind the Black Curtain* (Philadelphia, 1965), 33.
3. *Ibid.*, 35.
4. *Ibid.*, 36.

trial faculty and the curriculum had greatly improved. Most likely, Work went to Savannah with both a sense of mission and a qualified optimism. His new college was growing and prospering, and his new city seemed to be bucking the rising tide of racism. Perhaps his first disappointment was the lack of library facilities at the college. This did not dampen his growing enthusiasm for research, however. He quickly discovered that he could borrow source material from the Library of Congress. Out of a meager salary of eight hundred dollars a year, he began purchasing the bibliographic cards on Africa and became a subscriber to all future cards.[5]

Work also found an outlet for his research activities through a continuing participation in the Atlanta Studies. For the 1904 Atlanta Conference on the Negro and Crime, he prepared a statistical analysis of arrest and conviction records in a number of leading cities. He concluded that the black crime rate appeared to have been decreasing since 1894 and was about equal in the North and South, although higher in the cities of both regions. At the same conference Work also read a paper comparing black crime in Savannah and Chicago.[6]

Later, in an effort to offset the impact of studies that purported to prove the Negro brain smaller and structurally inferior to the white brain, Work contributed a memorandum to the 1906 Atlanta Study of the Health and Physique of the Negro American. In this memorandum he pointed out the inadequacies of studies that were based on haphazard research methods, including the use of too few samples and the neglect of such variables as age, stature, occupation, nutrition, and cause of death.[7]

In addition to the Atlanta Studies, Work cooperated in a number of other research projects with Du Bois, who appeared convinced of Work's abilities and offered him generous compensation for his help. Work also devoted significant attention to the annual Farm-

5. Monroe N. Work, "Making a Bibliography" (Typescript, n.d., in Box 1, Monroe Nathan Work Papers, Tuskegee Institute Archives).

6. Monroe N. Work, "Crime in the Cities," in W. E. B. Du Bois (ed.), Negro Crime, Atlanta University Publications, No. 9 (Atlanta, 1904), 18–32, 64.

7. Monroe N. Work, "The Negro Brain," in W. E. B. Du Bois (ed.), The Health and Physique of the Negro American, Atlanta University Publications, No. 11 (Atlanta, 1906), 25–27.

ers' Conferences, and in the summer of 1906 he toured the state in support of the Colored State Fair. During this period, too, he published a number of articles on Africa in the *Southern Workman*, which established him as a pioneer in African studies.[8]

Work found much intellectual stimulation from his contacts outside Savannah, but he also soon entered the social life of his new city. He lived in an antebellum mansion on campus that was reputed to have been built with the proceeds of the last load of slaves brought from Africa to Georgia. There he met and mingled with other faculty members. He and three other instructors at the college conducted an informal tennis match with the results being carried tongue-in-cheek by the local black newspaper.[9]

In Savannah, Work also met his future wife, Florence E. Hendrickson, a public school teacher from one of the city's leading black families. Their marriage on December 27, 1904, marked the beginning of a long and happy partnership. Throughout forty-one years of marriage, Florence Work remained totally blind to any fault in her husband, and Work was devoted to his wife, who was almost as quiet and reserved as he. The only blights on the union were Florence's frequent illnesses and the death of all their children in infancy. The void resulting from the loss of their own children was largely filled, however, by warm relationships with several nieces and nephews who lived with the Works from time to time.[10]

As Monroe Work's involvement in the city grew, he became aware that the bright promise for black advancement was not being adequately fulfilled. Race relations were somewhat more cordial and less violent than elsewhere, but Savannah blacks were nevertheless victims of a paternalistic tokenism that placed them in a clearly subordinate position. Although 54 percent of the city's 72,000 residents were black in 1906, the whites exercised a firm, if

8. W. E. B. Du Bois to Monroe Work, July 17, 1906, August 10, 1905, both in Box 2, Work Papers; Jessie P. Guzman, "Monroe Nathan Work and His Contributions," *Journal of Negro History*, XXXIV (October, 1949), 434; August Meier, *Negro Thought in America, 1880–1915* (Ann Arbor, 1963), 313–14.

9. Savannah *Tribune*, November 11, December 17, 1904.

10. Jessie P. Guzman, my interview, January 6, 1982.

benevolent, control over the black majority. Of the city officials, only the caretaker of the "colored section" of the city cemetery and two of the four city physicians were black. They held the three posts allotted to blacks by law. This dearth of black officials was due in part to the unofficial discrimination of the voter registrars. Of two hundred blacks who attempted to register during the last week of July, 1906, only twenty-six were added to the voting rolls. As the white city newspaper noted, "In all cases where it was apparent that the applicant was trying to impose on the registrar and beat down the county, he was turned down." Thus the voters registered that year included 6,937 whites and only 501 blacks.[11]

The limits of paternalism can be found elsewhere in the pages of the white newspaper as well. When Tuskegee Institute celebrated its twenty-fifth anniversary, an editorial criticized the celebrants for not openly denying any need for black suffrage. On another occasion, the newspaper reported a judge's speech before a grand jury, in which he castigated blacks who tried to improve conditions for the masses and declared, "If the best class [of Negroes] feels an obligation to fight for education and opportunity, for all classes of negroes, they should fight equally hard against their vice and crime."[12]

Savannah blacks could be justifiably proud of their success in blocking legal segregation until 1906, but even before its enactment, they were hardly free to go anywhere they wished in the city. The lack of legal definition created a confusing hodgepodge of local custom. Some private institutions and facilities served all equally, some admitted blacks but segregated them, and others totally excluded blacks.

The most devastating form of segregation was in the schools, for the county board of education discriminated against the black schools. In 1906, 131 white teachers were paid a total of $86,900 to teach 5,256 white students, but only 70 black teachers, allotted a total of $23,500, were expected to teach 4,224 black children.

11. Savannah, Georgia, *Municipal Reports, 1906* (Savannah, 1907), 7–8, 164; *The Code of the City of Savannah of 1907* (Savannah, 1907), Chap. 42, Sec. 967, Chap. 58, Sec. 1251; Savannah *Morning News*, July 1, 1906.

12. Savannah *Morning News*, April 7, December 4, 1906.

The following year, $4,200 was appropriated for the white library and $360 for the black one. It is hardly any wonder that Monroe Work developed a lifelong interest in the funding for black public schools.[13]

Work's interest in black health was also stimulated by conditions in Savannah. The poorer blacks lived in unsanitary conditions, suffered from malnutrition, and lacked adequate access to health care. The result was a startlingly high death rate; white births exceeded deaths by 245, but among blacks the figure was only 10. The city health officer found the statistics alarming, and he made an eloquent plea for white action in his 1906 annual report. Although he was probably the most ardent white champion of the "black cause" that year, he was not free of the paternalism infecting the white elite. He declared, "The negro is with you for all time. He is what you will make him and it is 'up' to the white people to prevent him from becoming a criminal and to guard him against Tuberculosis, Syphilis, etc."[14]

While Monroe Work undoubtedly supported such white actions, he also believed that the black elite shared responsibility for the condition of the masses. By 1905 he had perhaps realized the limits of white paternalism and drew on his Chicago experiences to find a vehicle for black action. Thus he provided the leadership for the formation of the Savannah Men's Sunday Club on April 16, 1905. It was announced that the club would meet every Sunday afternoon at 4:30 in the Masonic Temple to explore conditions of "vital importance to the life and progress of the colored citizen." The club offered an opportunity to those blacks whose "trainings have fitted them for this great work" to "come from their closets of seclusion and lift up those who are dying in the most pitiable of surroundings."[15]

Under Work's leadership as the club's first president, it grew rapidly in membership and influence. By the end of the first year, over three hundred men had joined, and the club was conducting a

13. Georgia Department of Education, *Thirty-fifth Annual Report from the Department of Education to the General Assembly of the State of Georgia* (Atlanta, 1907), 402–14; *Municipal Reports, 1906,* 9.
14. *Municipal Reports, 1906,* 155, 164.
15. Savannah *Tribune,* April 22, May 27, 1905.

wide variety of service projects and cultural programs. There were no membership restrictions, but the leadership of the Sunday Club was mainly composed of the kind of college-educated professional men whom Du Bois had labeled the Talented Tenth. S. P. Lloyd, the vice-president, was a medical doctor who had graduated from Atlanta University and the University of Pennsylvania. In addition to a number of instructors at Georgia State Industrial College, active members included J. Walter Williams, another doctor; Charles McDowell, a graduate of Fisk University; J. W. Armstrong, the manager of the Metropolitan Realty Company; and E. W. Houstoun, a graduate of Atlanta University who later became an instructor in Mathematics at Lincoln Institute in Jefferson City, Missouri. Typically, the so-called Talented Tenth who participated in the Sunday Club actually composed only .5 percent of Savannah's total black population.[16]

In keeping with its professed ideals, the club initiated a number of programs to improve the conditions of the black masses. In an effort to bring down the appalling death rate among the lower classes, members of the club went to the black churches of Savannah to teach sanitation and to dispel superstitious health practices. Mothers' Clubs were formed to teach proper infant and child care. A committee was named to establish day nurseries. The Sunday Club joined with a women's group to raise ten thousand dollars for the erection of a modern annex to Charity Hospital. Although some of the projects apparently failed and no spectacular decline in the death rate occurred, the club had at least helped make both races more aware of the problem in the city. This movement was also a forerunner of the much more extensive National Negro Health Week program, in which Work was later to play a principal role.[17]

In the same spirit of extending a helping hand to the less fortunate, the Sunday Club sponsored programs of slum work and sought to deal with the problem of crime among blacks in Savan-

16. *Ibid.*, Feburary 17, 1906.

17. Monroe N. Work, "A Health Week in Savannah, Georgia, in 1905" (Typescript in Box 2, Work Papers); Savannah *Tribune*, June 17, July 22, October 28, June 3, 10, 1905.

nah, attacking such evils as the policy shops and dives. To reach all sections of the community, a ladies' auxilliary and a junior division were organized. The ladies' auxilliary met during the week and occasionally presented the program on Sunday. The women also administered the junior division, which functioned like a scouting program.[18]

In addition to offering its members an opportunity to serve, the Sunday Club provided a medium of cultural and intellectual exchange. Members shared their specialized knowledge with the club and presented programs on a wide range of subjects, including the development of the English language and astronomy. Several programs were dedicated to black music and a Coleridge Taylor Glee Club was formed.

Late in 1905 the Sunday Club decided to make its cultural activities more available to the general public. A lecture series was established with ten programs scheduled between November, 1905, and May, 1906. For the price of a one-dollar season ticket, the holder was entitled to hear a number of outstanding blacks, including W. E. B. Du Bois, H. H. Proctor, a leading clergyman from Atlanta, and F. J. Work, the renowned musician from Fisk University. So enthusiastic was the response that on the club's first anniversary a public reading room was opened to further cultural growth in the community.[19]

Underlying the cultural crusade of the Sunday Club was the desire to illustrate the accomplishments of blacks and to inspire self-respect. The club's promotion of racial solidarity and cooperation complemented these efforts. Dr. S. P. Lloyd stressed the necessity for blacks to stop discriminating among themselves if they wished discrimination by whites to cease. R. H. Boyd addressed the club regarding the National Baptist Publishing House, an organization he had founded to provide blacks with their own Sunday school literature because the white American Baptist Publication Society refused to accept contributions from Negroes. The club also sent

18. Savannah *Tribune*, June 2, 1906, October 28, August 12, June 3, December 23, 1905, May 5, 1906.

19. *Ibid.*, July 7, January 20, 1906, July 29, November 11, 1905, April 28, 1906.

teams to the black churches to preach the doctrines of racial solidarity and patronage—an effort later described as instrumental in
the propagation of a number of new black-owned businesses.[20]

All of these activities were part of the civic-cultural nature of
the club and were similar to the programs advocated by Booker T.
Washington. Indeed, this similarity was undoubtedly a factor in
Work's later response to the Tuskegean. In 1905, however, Work's
association with W. E. B. Du Bois was strengthening at the very
time the rift between Du Bois and Washington was widening.

An expanding group of black intellectuals, Du Bois among them,
had become concerned over the dictatorial methods that Washington had adopted to maintain his position of leadership among
blacks. Washington's control of white philanthropic funds and political patronage and his subsidization of segments of the black
press gave him a great deal of power to quiet any dissension over
his accommodationist program. At times he used this power quite
ruthlessly.

Not only did Du Bois object to Washington's methods of leadership, he was also increasingly discontented with the effectiveness
of Washington's approach to the growing problems of the Afro-
American. Although the two men secretly cooperated in several
civil rights activities, Du Bois believed that Washington's public
acquiescence to the white South and his disdain of higher education had done great injustice to the black cause. Du Bois made
these feelings public in *The Souls of Black Folk*, published in 1903.

After a few unsuccessful attempts at rapprochement with Washington, Du Bois joined with William Monroe Trotter in 1905 to
found a movement to counter the influence of Washington and to
take a more vigorous stand for civil rights. In order to establish a
national strategy board for the Niagara Movement, as it came to be
called, they decided to invite a "few selected persons" to secret sessions that summer. One of these was Monroe Work.[21]

20. *Ibid.*, August 5, 1905 (issue dated July 29 by mistake), July 28, 1906; Savannah *Journal*, February 28, 1920 (Clipping in Box 2, Work Papers).
21. See Elliott Rudwick, "The Niagara Movement," *Journal of Negro History*, XLII (July, 1957), 177–200.

Although Du Bois contended that the Niagara Movement was dedicated to principles rather than personalities, his anti-Washington bias could clearly be seen in a letter to Monroe Work regarding the 1905 conference. Du Bois proposed the following as the purposes of the conference:

> 1. To oppose firmly the present methods of strangling honest criticism, manipulating public opinion, and centralizing political power by means of the improper and corrupt use of money and influence.
> 2. To organize thoroughly the intelligent and honest Negroes through the United States for the purpose of insisting on manhood rights, industrial opportunity and spiritual freedom.
> 3. To establish and support proper organs of news and public opinion.[22]

Apparently Work was in sympathy with these principles for he attended the July conference at Niagara Falls, serving as a member of the Committee on Interstate Conditions and Needs and as secretary of the Committee on Crime, Rescue, and Reform. The following October, John Hope, the Georgia state secretary of the Niagara Movement, became ill, and Du Bois asked Work to fill his position.[23]

Work had established the Savannah Men's Sunday Club in the same month he was corresponding with Du Bois about the Niagara Movement, and his links to the so-called radicals were clearly seen in some of the club's activities. Having witnessed the subordination of Savannah blacks in an atmosphere of accommodation and complacency, many of the college-educated leaders of the club supported the Niagara Movement and insisted on full manhood rights. The movement's program and principles were discussed at club meetings, and reflecting the spirit of the Niagara Movement, the Sunday Club also sought to increase the political effectiveness of blacks in Savannah. Committees were formed to campaign for the payment of the poll tax by the lower classes. In order to meet objec-

22. Du Bois to Work, April 25, 1905, in Box 2, Work Papers.
23. List of Committees of the Niagara Movement, n.d., Du Bois to Work, October 23, 1905, both in Box 2, Work Papers.

tions to the payment of the tax, programs were presented to show how widespread payment could benefit blacks.[24]

Summarizing one of these programs, a writer in the black newspaper expressed his distress that Savannah's black majority made up only 10 percent of the voting rolls. Those offering such excuses as "Why should I pay, when the primary system is so largely put into operation?" and "I haven't any children, why should I pay to educate other men's children?" were labeled as "dodgers," willing to give up without a fight. The pressure that a large body of registered black voters could place on the politicians and the board of education was sufficient reason for paying the necessary dollar a year. In a postscript the author quoted his dog, Napoleon, as saying that "men are made a little lower than the angels, but the fellow who doesn't pay his poll tax is less by far than a dog who wears a dollar license around his neck."[25]

Another member of the Sunday Club, Samuel Grant, delivered a speech entitled "The Negro as a Political Factor," in which he attacked political apathy among blacks. Grant was dismayed by those who sold their votes and by the blind adherence of the race to the Republican party. By consistently delivering their votes to one party, said Grant, Negroes had negated the need to cater to their voting power and had become "mere parasites to the Republican party, human automatons, imitating them, but not demanding any rights from them." Grant believed blacks owed nothing to the Republican party, which had "made slaves freemen and freemen slaves in the same breath by conferring the franchise and withholding the guarantees to insure its exercise." Blacks could produce enough votes to sway most elections, and it was therefore time to "cease to be duped by one party and shot at by another." The duty of blacks was to strive to meet any qualifications unjustly placed on the franchise and, if necessary, to organize their own primaries.[26]

The Sunday Club's drive for equitable appropriations for black

24. Savannah *Tribune*, July 29, September 2, 1905, July 21, 1906, July 15, 1905.

25. *Ibid.*, February 10, 1906.

26. *Ibid.*, September 2, 1905.

education in Savannah was closely tied to the poll tax crusade. Since the receipts from the poll tax were earmarked for education, Savannah whites had justified the proportionately low educational expenditures for Negroes by the failure of blacks to pay the tax. Of course, as E. W. Houstoun argued in a speech before the club, blacks did pay property taxes in sufficient proportion to entitle them to a larger share than their schools were receiving. By use of several charts, Houstoun illustrated how far black schools lagged behind white ones in facilities, teachers, principals' salaries, and class size. His speech was probably motivated by the recent decision of the board of education to condemn and tear down a white school that blacks felt was in better condition than any of their existing schools. The prevailing attitude of the club regarding education was best expressed by H. H. Proctor, minister of the First Congregational Church in Atlanta, who delivered the first talk in the Sunday Club's lecture series on November 14, 1905. "If the black man is equal to the white," he said, "then give him the same education; if inferior then a superior education; if superior then an inferior education."[27]

No aspect was ignored in the Sunday Club's consideration of the discrimination that blacks faced in Savannah. In his lecture, "The Duty of the Hour," Proctor argued that "one man's rights should not be sacrificed for another's prejudices." It was time, he said, for blacks to recognize and assert their rights—including the "right to life" and the "right to expect to be treated like men." The right to life should not be denied anyone without due process of law, yet the evil of lynching was growing stronger every year. Proctor declared that "in a land of religious, intellectual, and political freedom there should also be social freedom." Yet when Booker T. Washington and a white man had dined together by mutual assent, a public uproar resulted. What the South needed, said Proctor, was "right supremacy" instead of "white supremacy."[28]

The evils of lynching and Jim Crow cars were iterated in a

27. *Ibid.*, July 1, December 9, 1905.
28. *Ibid.*, December 9, 1905.

speech by E. W. Houstoun. The Sunday Club leaders obviously supported his attack on segregated facilities, for they sent resolutions of commendation to the blacks of Jacksonville, Florida, supporting their boycott of the new Jim Crow streetcars in the city. It is clear that all through the first year and a half of the club's existence, its members took an aggressive stand for full manhood rights.[29]

The year 1906, however, had a profound impact on both the club and its founder and president, Monroe Work. The year brought racial tensions all across the South with several outbreaks of violence, as at Brownsville, Texas, in August and Atlanta, Georgia, in September. In Atlanta twenty-five blacks were killed by white mobs that stopped streetcars and broke into houses to attack blacks. At the same time Savannah witnessed a changing pattern of race relations.[30]

One reason for the racial massacre in Atlanta was the arousal of white prejudice by the bitter Negrophobe gubernatorial campaign of Hoke Smith. All across Georgia, Smith preached that "reform" demanded the exclusion of Negroes from both politics and social contact with whites. Savannah whites began to express the feeling that their city was behind the times and should get in step with this reform movement. During the first six months of 1906, this sentiment was reflected in numerous minor disturbances: two Negroes were sentenced to pay fifty dollars or spend thirty days in jail for jeering at a white man in a parade; a black man was illegally expelled from the courthouse for sitting in a "white folk's seat"; the president of the city board of education forced teachers to use a racially derogatory paraphrase of the song "Dixie"; and no charges were brought against a white streetcar operator who attacked a Negro.[31]

29. *Ibid.*, November 11, July 29, 1905.
30. Charles Crow, "Racial Massacre in Atlanta, September 22, 1906," *Journal of Negro History*, LIV (April, 1969), 150–73.
31. Charles Crow, "Racial Violence and Social Reform: Origins of the Atlanta Riot of 1906," *Journal of Negro History*, LIII (July, 1968), 234–56; Savannah *Morning News*, September 11, 18, 1906; Savannah *Tribune*, January 13, March 17, May 5, June 28, 1906.

Tension was definitely in the air, but there was no basis for serious alarm by either race until July, 1906, when black stevedores began a strike against the firm of Smith and Kelley. The city government reacted by requesting state troopers and applying vagrancy laws to harass the strikers. Soon the vagrancy campaign was extended to bring all the black labor force "into line," as was being done in Macon, Augusta, and Atlanta. One black was picked up for vagrancy while sitting in his own home, and bond was refused for several who were arrested. The editor of Savannah's black newspaper considered it strange that there were few or no white vagrants and that the state troopers were unable to control the white mobs intimidating the Negro strikers.[32]

As a result of the increased racial tension and the desire of a large number of whites to get into the "new order of things," Savannah passed its first lasting Jim Crow law on September 12, 1906. The law required separate seating in streetcars and empowered the police to arrest anyone sitting in the wrong place. Immediately a streetcar boycott was organized, and blacks were urged to save their money and walk. While one group of blacks attempted to form the United Transportation Company in competition with the white lines, blacks were beseeched to remain patient, for surely "some day the people will get tired of hearing about the Negro and will not allow so many demagogic fellows to ride into office on this hobbyhorse."[33]

The strike and boycott had a great impact on the Sunday Club. For three months—from July 28, the week the strike began, until October 27—there was no mention of the club's activities in the Savannah *Tribune*, which had previously reported its meetings weekly. What had happened? Had those men who had publicly praised the boycott in Jacksonville suddenly changed their minds? This seems unlikely, since a large number of the Sunday Club's leaders joined with other groups to protest the new conditions in

32. Savannah *Tribune*, July 28, August 4, 1906; Crow, "Racial Violence," 247.

33. *Code of Savannah, 1907*, Chap. 55, Secs. 1194–1198; Savannah *Tribune*, September 9, 29, 1906.

Savannah. With others, they wrote Judge Samuel B. Adams for a clear definition of the vagrancy laws, drafted a protest against the proposed Jim Crow law, and formed the United Transportation Company.[34]

Why did the members of a club that had repeatedly taken a stand for full manhood rights have to channel their activities through other groups to protest the infringement of these rights? The answer is perhaps found by considering which group of the Sunday Club's leadership did not overtly enter into any of the protest movements. A number of instructors at Georgia State Industrial College had played a conspicuous role in founding and operating the Sunday Club. Included in this group was the club's president, Monroe Work. Yet not one of these men joined any of the newly formed protest groups. There were no fundamental differences between them and the club members who were protesting, with one exception: they were employed by the state of Georgia. This fact provided a means of pressure, which seemingly was used very effectively.[35]

The Sunday Club's first reported meeting after the strike reflected a need for some kind of reorganization and restatement of principles. A column in the Savannah *Tribune* announced that the club would meet on October 28 to "discuss the different features of its work and plan for same" and to consider the resignation of President Work. At that time S. P. Lloyd apparently assumed the presidency, but Work continued to participate in the club's activities until he left Savannah almost two years later.[36]

Whether or not Work willingly refrained from the protest activities in Savannah in 1906, during the following two years he witnessed the failure of protest to stem the tide of segregation in Savannah and saw the virtual collapse of the Niagara Movement. Work's few years in Savannah had taught him something about the complexities of black life in the South. He came to realize that simplistic approaches could not solve problems that were rooted in

34. Savannah *Tribune*, August 18, September 9, 29, 1906.
35. *Georgia State Industrial College Catalog, 1905–1906*, 6; Savannah *Tribune*, August 18, September 9, 29, 1906.
36. Savannah *Tribune*, October 27, 1906, February 2, 1907, July 25, 1908.

educational, economic, environmental, and political situations. All that he had experienced reaffirmed his belief in the necessity of more factual data to help unravel the intricate and confusing conditions that held his people at the bottom of American society. Although Work never rejected protest as a legitimate method of racial advancement, he determined not to let it handicap his efforts as a sociologist for the benefit of the race. At the fork of the road, Monroe Work chose the path that led to Tuskegee.

III / The Center of Things
Relating to the Negro

Monroe Work's life had reached a crossroads even before Booker T. Washington's invitation to come to Tuskegee Institute. Not only had he witnessed the failure of protest in Savannah, but he was also aware that a disillusioned Du Bois had begun moving from scholarship toward propaganda. Du Bois' transition came at the very time that Work was beginning to conceptualize his own role in the quest for black advancement. Work realized that he most certainly was not an orator; his attempts at preaching and teaching had met with little success. His two great assets were his analytical mind and his trained research skills. Thus, the question he faced in 1908 was how his abilities could best be utilized.

Certainly, remaining at Savannah would be a poor choice. Work's meager salary and the lack of library facilities hampered his research, and teaching took up much of his time. He wanted a position where he would have adequate funding and, preferably, be freed from the burden of teaching. He also needed some vehicle for the dissemination of his findings.

Meanwhile, at Tuskegee Normal and Industrial Institute, Booker T. Washington realized that he needed more accurate information to wage his battles for his race and for his school. Close friends advised him that the great demands placed upon him for speeches and articles required a trustworthy source of factual data. If his facts were successfully challenged, his effectiveness as a black spokesman would be diminished. Moreover, in order to campaign successfully for funds and to continue developing the institute's program, he needed to know what the school and its graduates were accomplishing in society. He needed accurate statistics to demonstrate the value of Tuskegee's efforts. In addition, Washington had long harbored a vague desire to introduce sociological studies of some sort at his school, perhaps because a rival institution, Atlanta University, had such a program. Indeed, in 1899, he had asked Du Bois to establish a sociological research program at Tuskegee. Du Bois' decision to remain in Atlanta dramatically affected the course of history and left a void at Tuskegee. By 1908 Washington and his advisors believed it was time to fill that void.[1]

In an executive council meeting in Tuskegee on May 19, 1908, it was decided to hire a man to "study the work of the school and graduates with reference to what they are doing for society, and to collect and classify data which will be of general value and interest." Two people were mentioned as suitable for the job: a Tuskegee faculty member and Monroe Work.[2] On the surface it seems odd that the name of Monroe Work, a member of the enemy camp, should have come up at all.

Undoubtedly Washington was hypersensitive to criticism; his aggressive tactics against those who opposed him illustrate his inability to tolerate competition. He had begun to view his personal success and that of all Afro-Americans as synonymous. Because of the publicity generated by his every action, he believed that whatever reflected badly upon him hurt the race as a whole. Certainly he viewed the members of Du Bois' Niagara Movement as enemies of his cause, and since his partisans had infiltrated the movement, it is unlikely that he was unaware of Monroe Work's involvement. Yet Washington, a relatively uneducated man, had won his success through his great abilities at administration and politics. Armed with only a diploma from an industrial school, Hampton Institute, and a two-thousand-dollar state appropriation, he had come to Macon County in 1881 to establish a school for blacks. Within twenty years he had garnered for Tuskegee Institute the second

1. Monroe N. Work, interview by Lewis A. Jones, May 15, 1932 (Transcript in Box 1, Jessie P. Guzman Papers, Tuskegee Institute Archives), hereinafter cited as Jones interview; Booker T. Washington to W. E. B. Du Bois, October 26, 1899, in Box 282A, Booker T. Washington Papers, Library of Congress.

2. Minutes of the Executive Council (Manuscript in Box 1007, Washington Papers), May 19, 1908.

largest endowment of any black school in the United States, behind only Hampton. He was above all else a realist and a pragmatist, and he knew he needed the best men available to help run the "Tuskegee Machine." Despite his human weaknesses, Washington sincerely desired to serve his race in the most effective manner possible, and the opportunities he provided to his able lieutenants, such as George Washington Carver, are among his greatest legacies.

While conducting a search for a qualified man, Washington had consulted two white sociologists who were his personal friends. Both these men had come into contact with Monroe Work and were greatly impressed with his abilities. Thomas Jesse Jones, at that time teaching sociology at Hampton Institute, had made a tour of black schools in the South. President Wright of Georgia State Industrial College, not wanting to be bothered, turned Jones's tour of that campus over to Work. Their long conversations convinced Jones that Work was a man of great potential. Robert E. Park, who was later to lead the sociology department at Chicago to the peak of its influence, lived in Tuskegee, where he was doing research and working with Washington on several books and articles. He attended the Georgia State Fair in 1906 and saw a display of statistical charts that Work had prepared. Impressed with the accuracy and clarity of the material, Park brought the charts to Washington's attention.[3]

On the basis of these high recommendations, Washington, the great administrator, decided to interview his former enemy. The week after the executive council meeting, the principal was to pass through Savannah on his way to Beaufort, South Carolina, where he was scheduled to deliver a speech. He wrote Work of his plans, "If possible, I want to have a conference with you in regard to a course in sociology and history, which I want to introduce into this Institution." Work wired his agreement to meet the principal, and their first meeting took place at 8:35 P.M., May 29, in a pullman car switched to a siding in Savannah. Monroe Work later recounted the brief conference.

3. Jones interview; Lewis A. Jones, my interview, May 2, 1972.

I went down to the car and said I wanted to see Mr. Washington. He was out in the open pullman. Mr. Scott came and stood by him. In general, whenever he was going to talk to anybody about anything that was important, his secretary was there. Mr. Scott would tell him the next day just what had happened.

This is what took place. I told him who I was. He nodded his head. I don't think he ever shook hands with me. I told him I came down in reply to his letter. He wanted to know where I had been educated and I told him. He wanted to know what I thought about his suggestion and I told him I would have to think it over. He then told me to come to Tuskegee and we would settle it.[4]

In spite of its brevity, the meeting seems to have made an impact on both men. The next day Work wrote for a Tuskegee catalog. On June 3 Washington announced to the executive council that Work "is considered favorably for the work of collecting information concerning work done by the school and the graduates and undergraduates of the institution." After that, the executive council had only to debate whether Work would be affiliated with the Division of History and Sociology or be classified as an administrator.[5]

Two days later Work arrived on campus and was impressed by the treatment he received. As he later noted, "Less than 30 days after I first saw [Booker T. Washington] I was [at Tuskegee] working." Obviously the attraction was mutual, for Washington offered Work twelve hundred dollars a year, a month's vacation, and a house. This was a large salary by Tuskegee's standards. Although most of the administrators were paid more, Work earned more than many division and department heads, including George Washington Carver.[6]

4. Washington to Monroe Work, May 22, 1908, Work to Washington, telegram, May 25, 1908, Washington to Work, May 28, 1908, all in Box 386, Washington Papers; "Mr. Work's Conference with Mr. Washington Concerning the Establishment of the Department of Records and Research" (Typescript, n.d., in Box 1, Guzman Papers).

5. Work to Washington, May 30, 1908, in Box 386, Washington Papers; Minutes of the Executive Council, June 3, 1908.

6. Minutes of the Executive Council, June 5, 1908; "Mr. Work's Conference"; Washington to Work, June 8, 1908, in Box 385, Washington Papers; Joseph F. Citro, *Booker T. Washington's Tuskegee Institute: Black School Community, 1900–1915* (Ann Arbor, 1973), 199–205, 210.

Work accepted the offer quickly, but the decision was probably a difficult one. For more than five years he had taken a stand against Washington's approach to the race problem. As an active member of the Niagara Movement, he had supported a more aggressive response to disfranchisement and segregation and had rejected Washington's emphasis on industrial education and his claims to exclusive race leadership. But what viable alternatives existed in 1908? By then the Niagara Movement had burned out and the National Association for the Advancement of Colored People had not yet risen from the ashes.

Perhaps more than any of the other members of the Talented Tenth who had joined with Du Bois, Monroe Work was a man with a foot in both camps. His childhood more closely paralleled Washington's, but his educational background ranked him with Du Bois. He supported both the need for economic and educational advancement and the drive to preserve and expand black civil and political rights. The major question was how his talents could best serve the overall cause.

The principal driving force in Work's life was neither accommodation nor protest; rather, it was an abiding faith in the "impact of fact." His main concern was to obtain the best possible outlet for the fruits of his research. Du Bois was losing interest in research in his push for protest and resistance, and the meager facilities and funds at Savannah not only limited the accumulation of facts but circumscribed their distribution as well. Looking to Tuskegee Institute, Work could not help but be impressed by the opportunities for research. In addition to receiving more adequate funding, he would be freed from the duties of teaching and allowed to devote himself almost entirely to research. And the data he collected could have a world audience, for at that time, as Work later stated, "There was no place quite like Tuskegee. You had world contacts in a day. . . . It was the center of things relating to the Negro."[7] With the added incentive of a one-third increase in salary, it seems inconceivable that he would have chosen differently.

Work's assessment of the Tuskegee Institute was no doubt cor-

7. Jones interview.

rect. Yet it is hard to conceive of a more unlikely site for such a center. Macon County was located in the heart of rural, black-belt Alabama, and Tuskegee was one of the smallest county seats in the state. In 1908 there was a large black population, but a white minority exercised both economic and political control. Most of the county's blacks lived bleak lives of dismal poverty. In the era following Reconstruction, however, the newly enfranchised black community had possessed limited but real political clout. Lewis Adams, a skilled craftsman, served as a spokesman for black interests, and in 1880 he made a deal with two white politicians—Colonel Wilbur F. Foster, who was seeking election to the state senate, and Arthur L. Brooks, a candidate for the state legislature. Adams agreed to deliver the black vote if Foster and Brooks would obtain a state appropriation for a local black school. All kept their promises, and Booker T. Washington was summoned in 1881.

The school's continued existence depended on Washington's ability to convince local whites that the institute was an asset to their community and did not threaten their vested interests. With some fancy political footwork the principal succeeded, although his ultimate goal was black economic independence, which was surely not in the whites' perceived interest. Appeasing the whites required some compromises. Southern racial etiquette, for example, was scrupulously observed. But as black political power waned, not to be resurrected until after World War II, Booker T. Washington and his Tuskegee machine became a new center of power. They were consulted by presidents and philanthropists and considered the voice of black aspirations by most of the white world.[8]

Soon after his arrival at Tuskegee on July 3, Work discovered that a number of obstacles blocked the development of the kind of research program he had envisioned when he accepted the offer. He settled into a guest room in a boys' dormitory and reported to Washington the following day. The principal led him into his office and also summoned the school treasurer, Warren Logan, and his

8. See Louis R. Harlan, *Booker T. Washington: The Making of a Black Leader, 1856–1901* (New York, 1972).

own brother, John H. Washington, who often served as a kind of second-in-command at Tuskegee. Work noticed and was somewhat surprised that Washington's powerful secretary, Emmett J. Scott, was not present.[9]

The newcomer suggested that what Washington needed was "information about what is taking place at the present with reference to the Negro," not some kind of "History Department of the Negro." However, Washington was evasive and shifted the conversation to a discussion of Work's salary and his duties of keeping records of Tuskegee graduates. Someone asked what name was to be given to his duties, and Work proposed "the Department of Records and Research." As he later noted, "The Records would take care of the information on the graduates and the Research would allow for other things."[10]

Although Work left the meeting believing his position had been clarified, he later wrote that the "three men were not in the habit of discussing things and so the people here never did find out what went on in that meeting." Thus, Scott and everyone else "got the idea that I came to establish a placement bureau." The fact that Work spent a week at Hampton Institute studying its record-keeping facilities before coming to Tuskegee reinforced this popular conception of his role.[11]

Work nevertheless remained optimistic and later wrote his wife a glowing account of his situation: "I am getting more and more into my work. I am a sort of central bureau for the school's activities. I have met today with Mr. Lee and the heads of the various academic departments to discuss a better method of keeping records of attendance. . . . I will meet Mr. Lee again soon to discuss teachers' reports, etc. All this is with reference to the student's records. I have had a number of the people who are doing extension work before me. Thus I come more and more into the inner workings of the school." But confusion continued concerning Work's duties, and various members of the faculty and staff interpreted his

9. "Mr. Work's Conference."
10. *Ibid.*
11. *Ibid.*; Work to Washington, June 24, 1908, in Box 386, Washington Papers.

role differently. The campus newspaper, presided over by Scott, described his duties as studying Tuskegee graduates and the effects of the school's extension work. Significantly, the article indicated that Work had attended the University of Chicago but did not mention his master's degree.[12]

For two months Work labored without a title, despite his requests for clarification. Finally, on September 7 he suggested to the executive council that his position be entitled director of the Department of Records and Research. Scott, however, seemed to feel that the term *department* conveyed too much status, and his recommended label of Division of Records and Research was adopted by the council. That still left Work's personal title at issue, but Scott skillfully avoided the question by simply listing the sociologist as "In Charge" of the division in the school's catalog.[13]

These conditions remained until 1919, when department status was granted and Work was named to the executive council. Despite his background and ability, he was affiliated with the institute for over ten years and made several requests before he was permitted to join the select group of administrators and faculty members who composed the council. The fact that Work was better educated than the average council member may have posed a threat to Scott's central position of influence with Washington. At any rate, it was only after Scott had left Tuskegee to join the War Department that Work was appointed to the inner circle of power in the school.

Indeed, Work rapidly learned that he would have to adjust to the internal power structure at Tuskegee and to accommodate himself to the demanding and authoritarian leadership of Booker T. Washington. He had a long talk with Daniel C. Smith, the auditor of Tuskegee Institute, whom he had known in Chicago. Smith described the inside workings of the institution, the difficulties Work might encounter, and "Mr. Washington's pecularities." Work also quickly realized that he would have to be aggressive in making a

12. Work to Florence Work, August 31, 1908 (Typed abstract in Box 1, Guzman Papers); Tuskegee *Student*, July 18, 1908.
13. Work to Washington, August 7, 1908, in Box 585, Minutes of the Executive Council (Box 1007), September 7, 8, 9, 1908, Work to Washington, March 28, 1912, in Box 630, all in Washington Papers.

place for himself at Tuskegee. Even the promised cottage was not made available immediately, and then the house assigned to the Works, an old nurses' cottage, proved unlivable. "It is too small," he wrote Washington. "We are compelled to cook and eat in the same room and are otherwise crowded. It has no toilet conveniences and because of its nearness to the engine house, we can not put up the windows without everything becoming covered with soot." Nevertheless, six months later the Works still had not received new quarters, and they remained dissatisfied with their housing arrangements until they bought their own home.[14]

Work also had problems acquiring adequate stenographic help. As early as August, 1908, he informed Scott that he needed help in transferring fifteen hundred student records to cards and was informed that there was no appropriation. He was forced to rely on student help, which did not always prove satisfactory, until 1910, when he was finally given a full-time stenographer. She remained his only staff, aside from students, until another clerk was added in 1917.[15]

The facilities and equipment provided for the Division of Records and Research were also often inadequate. Work considered his office too small for his own operation, and yet he was sometimes forced to share it with others. In addition, he was frequently allotted only one typewriter and was then asked to provide typing services for other divisions and people.[16]

These kinds of handicaps Work shared with his colleagues at Tuskegee Institute. Although the school was better endowed and financed than most black colleges, funds were still relatively mea-

14. Work to Florence Work, August 31, 1908 (Typed abstract in Box 1, Guzman Papers); Work to Washington, February 11, 1909, in Box 593, November 25, 1913, in Box 639, June 11, 1909, in Box 593, all in Washington Papers; Work to Robert R. Moton, October 3, 1916, in Box LC5, Robert Russa Moton Papers, Tuskegee Institute Archives; Minutes of the Executive Council (Manuscript in Tuskegee Institute Archives), April 20, 1917.

15. Work to Emmett J. Scott, August, 29, 1908, Scott to Work, September 1, 1908, Work to Washington, January 5, March 30, 1909, Washington to Work, May 25, 1909, all in Box 585, Washington Papers.

16. Washington to Work, October 8, 1913, in Box 639, Work to Washington, September 1, 1909, in Box 593, Work to Scott, October 26, 28, 1912, both in Box 630, all in Washington Papers.

ger for the great task Booker T. Washington had undertaken—to elevate an entire people who were considered incapable of advancement by the dominant white society that controlled the bulk of the available resources. Prior to the Civil War, it had been illegal to teach blacks to read and write in most southern states. During and after the war, Yankee schoolmistresses, sponsored by various missionary societies, had flocked to the South to bring knowledge to the freedmen. Their efforts were expanded with the establishment of public schools by several state governments during Reconstruction—sometimes at the insistence of black legislators, who realized that most freedmen considered land and education the two major keys to real freedom. But those noble beginnings of the effort to eradicate black illiteracy faded as northern reformers lost interest and disfranchisement decimated black political power. The inadequate funding remaining from the missionary societies and the government was partially offset by grants from philanthropic robber barons, such as Andrew Carnegie and John D. Rockefeller. Nevertheless, Monroe Work and thousands of black educators were forced, figuratively, to "make bricks without straw."[17]

The biggest problem Work faced was the restricted concept of his duties. His only announced tasks were to compile a record of the occupations of former students and to study what the institute's extension activities had done for the betterment of the Negroes in Macon County. While he intended to handle those chores effectively, Work's own perception of his role was far more expansive. Nevertheless, his first years at Tuskegee were filled with a lot of routine administrative chores. He was charged with keeping records on all Tuskegee graduates, as well as tracking down former students to ascertain their positions in society. Such tasks were time-consuming enough, but in addition, as an outgrowth of the record keeping, Work was called upon to recommend students for various jobs and to supply Emmett J. Scott, the editor

17. See Horace Mann Bond, *Negro Education in Alabama: A Study in Cotton and Steel* (Washington, 1939); Henry Allen Bullock, *A History of Negro Education in the South from 1619 to the Present* (New York, 1970); Donald Spivey, *Schooling for a New Slavery: Black Industrial Education, 1868–1915* (Westport, Conn., 1978).

of the Tuskegee *Student,* with information on graduates. He was also given miscellaneous chores, which included supervising the delivery of photographs and even shoes. As more and more administrative demands were placed upon Work, occasional friction developed between him and Scott, who felt that the records in Work's charge were more important than his research efforts.[18]

The dedication and determination that had carried Work through many difficult times in the acquisition of his master's degree would not allow him to give up easily. His career was his whole life, and when more demands were placed upon him, he drew from his seemingly bottomless reservoir of energy. Time was precious to Work, and he wasted as little of it as possible. His home was both a retreat for the refreshment of his mind and body and a place to continue his work. His wife not only freed him from all household responsibilities but aided his research by reading through various materials and marking what he needed to see. One colleague remembered frequently passing by the house at night and seeing both of them sitting under a lamp reading. In addition, Florence Work actively participated in the larger research projects. The couple tended to view even their recreational activities—which included gardening, playing bridge, whist, and pinochle, and attending athletic events and the movies—as necessary means of renewal and relaxation to increase their vitality for their work.[19]

Both of the Works keenly felt the loss of all their children in infancy. Monroe loved children. He recalled with fond amusement how little children in Germany, who had never seen a brown man, would run behind him to stare, and he was pleased when the children of relatives visited. One of Florence's nieces lived with them for several years while she attended school in Tuskegee and later affectionately recalled their role as "second parents." Others of Florence's kin visited or lived with them for shorter periods of

18. Scott to Work, December 17, 1909, in Box 593, Work to Scott, September 25, 1913, Work to Washington, n.d., both in Box 639, all in Washington Papers.

19. Jessie P. Guzman, my interview, January 6, 1982; Jessie P. Guzman, "Monroe Nathan Work and His Contributions," *Journal of Negro History,* XXXIV (October, 1949), 458–60.

Monroe and Florence Work

time, but Monroe's family was more scattered and distant, and only one of his own nephews ever visited.[20]

The only other blight on the Works' very close relationship was Florence's frailty and her repeated illnesses. Monroe was solicitous of her. He made sure she always had help in running the house and someone to stay with her when he was out of town. On at least one occasion, Florence Work was not expected to live because of complications arising from a ruptured appendix. Despite her ill health, however, she was to outlive her husband by almost a decade.[21]

Both of the Works found their purpose in Monroe's work. Florence's support enabled him to devote his life to his career. Nothing better illustrates the untiring and wholehearted way in which Work approached any task that was given him than the following excerpt from a letter to Booker T. Washington from Robert E. Park, who was helping the principal write a book.

> I think I ought, now as "The Story of the Negro" is off our hands, to say something of the way in which Mr. Work has helped me during this long, tedious, and often very discouraging task. From the very first, although the work I was doing was not anything he felt responsible for and although the demands I made upon him often interfered with his own work, he has never shirked or complained. He has met every demand I made upon him in perfect cheerfulness, and has done the work I asked him to do, as faithfully as if he were working at some task of his own choosing, and according to his own methods and ideas.
>
> When I called upon him at the end of August to help me, he had already planned to take a week's vacation and was in the midst of moving his household goods. . . . He gave up that without a murmur and went to work. . . . For three or four days, he worked steadily from seven o'clock in the morning until ten o'clock at night without a stop except for meals, and at a kind of labor about as exhausting as I could well imagine. I have undertaken to write you in detail in regard to Mr. Work because I think the qualities he has shown are so rare and so they deserved to be recognized.[22]

20. Guzman interview; Mrs. P. H. Stone to author, July 28, 1972.

21. Eunice Rivers Laurie, interview by James H. Jones, May 3, 1977 (Transcript in the possession of Jones).

22. Robert E. Park to Washington, October 18, 1909, copy in Box 1, Monroe Nathan Work Papers, Tuskegee Institute Archives.

A quiet, reserved man who could only rarely be stirred to display fierce anger, Work was methodical in his work as well as his personal life, heavily scheduling his day. He would work at a task persistently and with painstaking perfectionism until it was completed in the best possible manner.

Work's employees quickly learned that what he demanded of himself, he expected of them also. On one occasion an assistant was asked three times to redo a chart she was compiling for one of Work's speeches. Unable to satisfy him, she finally gave up and told him to do it himself. He apologized the next day and informed her that the chart would be all right. Such perfectionism could be exasperating, but most of his employees, like this one, were caught up in his enthusiasm and willingly worked long, hard hours when necessary. Those who worked with him generally grew to love and respect Monroe Work, often seeking his advice on personal as well as professional problems. One remembered him as "more like a father than a boss." But Work was a hard taskmaster and expected those under him to do and to be their best, even down to good personal grooming. Sometimes his insistence on accuracy and efficiency provoked even his most admiring employees and sent those not willing to work to other departments. One female secretary even attacked him physically, clawing and calling him names. But by and large, Work's methods and manner produced a competent and productive department.[23]

Work's efficiency allowed him to meet the administrative demands placed upon him and still begin collecting the data and references that later resulted in the *Negro Year Book* and *A Bibliography of the Negro in Africa and America*. He also found time to conduct independent research projects that were published in various journals. As Work proved his ability and conscientiousness, Booker T. Washington and others turned more and more to him for help in a number of areas.

Washington soon realized that he could depend on Work to

23. Guzman interview; Work to Scott, January 14, 1915, in Box 664, Washington Papers.

quickly obtain any information he needed for his speeches or articles. Work supplied him with facts on such diverse topics as the rate of increase of black farmers, Negro migration to the cities, Negro crime, and education in Alabama for speeches that were made all over the United States. Work was not just a fact finder, however; he was also an advisor. The kind of advice he gave Washington can be seen in his proposals for a presentation to be given in Atlanta in the summer of 1915. He suggested the topic "Good Will" and recommended stressing that the "first requisite of good will is to know the other person." Work claimed that blacks understood whites far better than whites knew blacks. The only way to remedy this was "for leaders of White and Black people in every community throughout the South to meet in conferences where face to face they can come to know each other and where, also, they can begin to cooperate for the common good." His proposal sounds like a blueprint for the Commission on Interracial Cooperation, which would be formed in Atlanta after World War I to combat lynching.[24]

After several years of service, Work began to write or revise a number of articles and some speeches for Washington. The principal would submit chapters of books, articles, and even letters to Work for his comments and revisions. At other times he asked Work to ghost-write articles for him and other faculty members. Sometimes this created problems when the hand of the real author was too apparent. On one occasion Scott notified Work, "Two or three teachers since reading the article in The Independent have stated that they knew you wrote the article because they had read some of the matter before it was printed."[25]

Work also apparently assumed personal responsibility for the accuracy of all articles and speeches emanating from Tuskegee. He occasionally called attention to factual errors by professors and

24. Work to Washington, November 18, 1911, in Box 614, July 17, 1914, n.d., both in Box 653, n.d., in Box 639, June 18, 1915, in Box 664, all in Washington Papers.
25. Washington to Work, May 3, 1911, Work to Washington, December 27, 1910, June 2, May 24, 1911, all in Box 614, March 16, 1910, in Box 604, Scott to Work, April 6, 1911, in Box 614, all *ibid.*

even Washington himself. Although his actions may have caused some resentment, the major impact was to increase the trust-worthiness of data coming from Tuskegee. Washington realized the advantage of having a trained statistician and sociologist on his staff whenever his facts were challenged. In 1913 a New York news-paper wondered, "This Washington . . . has a veritable head for fig-ures, but it will be interesting to know where he gets them." The response was a long article about Monroe Work's background and training.[26]

Because of the general reliability of Work's data, he was often called upon to answer letters of inquiry that came to Tuskegee Institute. Washington's prestige led many people to contact the school for all kinds of information relating to blacks. Sometimes Work personally answered the letters; sometimes he merely sup-plied the information. He was also recruited by his colleagues for a variety of services, including translating letters. In addition, Washington frequently asked him for background information on cities where he was to speak. Work became a virtual fount of information.[27]

Although Washington publicly eschewed political involvement by blacks, his advice on political matters was often sought or given without solicitation. Sometimes he asked for Work's opinion of such pending legislation as the proposed repeal of the Alabama temperance law in 1910, the possibility of state legislation to re-quire separate records of black and white taxable property, legisla-tion on convict-lease labor, and the impact on blacks of the Page bill before the United States Senate in 1912. At other times Wash-ington wanted advice about how the institute could best take ad-vantage of existing legislation. Occasionally, Work took the ini-tiative and urged Washington to act—as when he discovered errors

26. Work to Washington, November 28, 1910, in Box 604, Work to Scott, May 1, 1911, in Box 614, Work to Washington, September 24, 1915, in Box 664, all *ibid*. Indianapolis *Recorder*, September 30, 1913 (Clipping in Box 2, Work Papers).

27. Work to Washington, September 10, 1909, in Box 593, Work to Scott, Feb-ruary 11, 19, 1915, both in Box 664, Charles Fearing to Work, January 13, 1910, in Box 604, all in Washington Papers.

in the 1910 census of Macon County and persuaded the principal to ask for a recount, which turned up 515 additional people.[28]

Work obviously fulfilled one of his original assignments well: he provided accurate information on blacks for institute officials. His other announced duty was to study the role of Tuskegee graduates and the school's extension efforts. Essentially, he was to supply Washington and others with factual ammunition in the battle for financial aid and other kinds of support for the school. In this area he again proved to be diligent and productive.

He implemented such an efficient system of record keeping that some of its features were adopted by Hampton Institute. Not content simply to write letters to graduates of the institute, he exploited various sources to obtain information on alumni, and he devised still other avenues, including sending a school agent to visit them. He studied not only Tuskegee graduates but also those who had attended but did not graduate. The results were both encouraging and a little discouraging. He reported, for example, that no Tuskegee graduate had ever been convicted of a criminal offense and that most were homeowners. More than one-third of the graduates were teachers, and there were approximately twenty physicians, eight lawyers, and twenty ministers in the alumni ranks as of 1909. Most of the others were directly or indirectly following the trades for which they had been trained. The status of former students who had not earned certificates was not quite as rosy. In comparison with graduates, fewer were engaged in teaching and twice as many worked for wages rather than for themselves. There was some cause for concern about the low number who were farming, for Tuskegee was supposed to be an agricultural school, and Washington decided that fact should not be publicized. The failure of many former students to directly pursue the trade for which they were trained was also embarrassing. Nevertheless, Work maintained, former Tuskegee students earned approximately seven hundred dollars a year, four hundred dollars more than the average black. Considering the impoverished background of many of the

28. Washington to Work, November 9, 21, 1910, Work to Washington, November 18, 1910, all in Box 604, Work to Washington, February 21, 28, 1911, both in Box 614, Washington to Work, February 28, 1912, in Box 625, all *ibid.*

school's students, these were indeed encouraging statistics, and Work proposed publishing them in pamphlet form.[29]

In the spring of 1910, he was given approval for such a pamphlet, which was to include data on the smaller schools that had been established by Tuskegee graduates. He was also requested to compile information for another publication on the results of the Tuskegee Negro Farmers' Conference. While tackling those chores, he suggested two additional projects: a pamphlet on the Tuskegee-sponsored National Negro Business League and an alumni directory. The idea for the directory was never approved, and Work was asked to concentrate on the distribution of the first pamphlet, which was published the following spring as *Industrial Work of Tuskegee Graduates and Former Students*. Some five thousand copies were printed and made available for thirty-five cents each plus seven cents postage.[30]

The concluding chapter of the booklet, entitled "The Value of an Industrial Education," clearly indicated that Monroe Work had become more than merely Washington's employee; he was a disciple. His conversion to the "Tuskegee idea" seemed complete, for in addition to stressing the economic value of Tuskegee's programs to the South, he asserted:

> The returns to the South from the training of these students are even greater than this. The Principal of Tuskegee Institute has always said, that in his opinion the greatest thing the school has done was to teach the dignity of labor. The persons who have gone out from Tuskegee Institute are leaders. They have spread the doctrine of the dignity of labor. By their example they have exerted a profound influence upon the Negroes of the South. They have assisted in improving the moral condition of the people. In this way they have directly and indirectly helped to improve economic conditions; since discipline, sobriety, order, and better family life all tend to economic efficiency.[31]

29. Work to Washington, March 6, 1909, in Box 604, Work to Fearing, March 13, 1909, Work to Washington, August 12, 1909 (two letters), August 26, 1909, all in Box 593, all *ibid*.

30. Washington to Work, May 14, May 21 (two letters) 1910, all in Box 604, Scott to Work, March 4, 1911, in Box 614, all *ibid*.; Tuskegee *Student*, March 4, 1911.

31. *Industrial Work of Tuskegee Graduates and Former Students* (Tuskegee, 1911), 61.

It could not have been said better by Washington himself.

Work's new loyalties were also evident in the vigor with which he approached his other assigned duty, the documentation of the contributions of Tuskegee's extension work. Washington had long sought to expand the institute's influence beyond the boundaries of the campus and to help local blacks who could not afford to become full-time students. He was undoubtedly motivated by both a sincere concern for the impoverished blacks of Macon County and a recognition that their backwardness reflected poorly on the school. Beginning with informal carriage rides into the countryside, Washington had gradually expanded the outreach programs, which were invigorated by George Washington Carver's arrival in 1896. Eventually Tuskegee sponsored annual farmers' conferences, farmers' institutes, short courses in agriculture, a colored fair, a movable school, and an agricultural experiment station that conducted research and published bulletins to aid the "man farthest down." All these activities were chronicled by Monroe Work, who was obviously impressed by their effectiveness.[32]

Work published numerous articles detailing Tuskegee's efforts under such titles as "Self-Help Among the Negroes," "A Short Course for Farmers," and "Agricultural Training at Tuskegee Institute." Washington recognized and appreciated these articles. They reflected Work's growing belief in the importance of such programs to the future of blacks. On one occasion Work noted: "By getting these Negroes to take steps for their own improvement, Tuskegee has made a valuable contribution to methods of social amelioration. These people by their self-help are not only advancing themselves, but they are contributing to the general welfare and progress of their country. They promise a future for the Negro for which none need despair. Tuskegee through its extension work in this county has worked out a method by which throughout the South the Negroes may be made to advance instead of retard the general progress and development."[33]

32. See Linda O. McMurry, *George Washington Carver: Scientist and Symbol* (New York, 1981); Allen W. Jones, "The Role of Tuskegee Institute in the Education of Black Farmers," *Journal of Negro History*, LI (April, 1975), 252–67.
33. Monroe N. Work, "Self-Help Among the Negroes," *Survey*, August 7,

His conversion was as much to Booker T. Washington, the man, as to Tuskegee's programs. His admiration for the principal can be seen in articles Work wrote after Washington's death. In "Booker T. Washington, Pioneer," for example, Work eulogized Washington's vision and tried to explain its nature and scope. It was an apparent attempt to refute the simplistic charges of opportunism and needless compromise that were often leveled at Washington. Work cataloged specific contributions in a wide variety of areas and summarized the continued impact of programs established before the principal's death. Eight years later Work published another article in which he described the broad aims of Tuskegee Institute. He noted that Washington had sought to do more than just educate students. He had also attempted to supply the needs of blacks in general, needs that "to him appeared to be economic, educational, moral, religious, social, and political," Work declared. "Running through all of these was the ever-present and over-shadowing problem of race relations." Work asked, "How could the needs of the Negro be met and at the same time a better understanding between the races developed?" He answered that it was a problem "for a statesman rather than an educator," and he believed that Washington had been remarkably successful in both roles, given the depth of the problems.[34]

Monroe Work's respect for Washington arose in part from his interaction with the man. His personal and professional relationships with the principal were remarkably smooth, considering the demanding and authoritatian nature of the "master of the Tuskegee plantation," as Washington has been called. Compared to other Tuskegeans, such as Carver, Work received very few letters of rebuke from the principal and wrote very few letters of complaint or

1909, pp. 616–18; Monroe N. Work, "Agricultural Training at Tuskegee Institute," Montgomery *Journal*, May 31, 1915 (Clipping in Box 3, Work Papers); Washington to Work, April 19, 1909, Work to Washington, July 21, 1909, both in Box 593, Washington Papers; Monroe N. Work, "Extension Work Among the Negroes of Macon County, Alabama" (Typescript, n.d., in Box 3, Work Papers).

34. Monroe N. Work, "Booker T. Washington, Pioneer," *Journal of Social Forces*, III (January, 1925), 310–15; Monroe N. Work, "Tuskegee Institute: More Than an Educational Institution," *Journal of Educational Sociology*, VII (November, 1933), 197–205.

demand himself. The amicable relations between the two men may have been partially due to the fact that they shared qualities that others occasionally found irritating. Both were perfectionists. Washington noted even scraps of paper littering the campus in his notebook; Work requested that his office be cleaned every day, instead of every other day. Both were also indefatigable workers and expected others to be the same. Thus, Work complained about the uncooperative spirit of the library staff regarding his need to work after hours and his request for duplicate copies of newspapers.[35]

Another factor that made his relationship with Washington relatively harmonious was Work's willingness to accept orders. He almost always did what was asked without question and seldom challenged Washington's refusal to grant his own requests. There were very few issues on which Work remained adamant. One was the need for better living quarters, and another was his insistence that his department operate on a twelve-month basis in spite of cost-cutting measures being taken at the time. Washington was finally able to accommodate him on both matters, helping to cement Work's growing loyalty.[36]

Work's conversion to the Tuskegee idea is also apparent in his activities on campus. He attended most of the cultural and athletic events and became an officer in a number of faculty organizations, some of which were similar to the Sunday Club. In addition, he founded some new clubs, such as the Sociology Club, and made financial contributions to the school's work.[37]

Nevertheless, his loyalty to Washington and Tuskegee was not blind. He recognized that many problems existed at the institute and made proposals to rectify them. As early as 1910 he described

35. Washington to Work, January 21, 1910, in Box 604, n.d., in Box 653, Work to Fearing, February 2, 1912, in Box 630, Work to Washington, July 8, 1914, in Box 653, all in Washington Papers.

36. Work to Washington, May 21, 1913, in Box 639, May 27, 1914, in Box 652, Washington to Work, June 4, 1914, in Box 652, November 27, 1914, in Box 653, Work to Washington, July 17, 1915, in Box 664, all *ibid*.

37. Tuskegee *Student*, December 19, 1908, February 4, 1911, August 27, 1921; Tuskegee *Messenger*, May 29, 1926; Work to Washington, January 4, 1911, in Box 614, Washington Papers; Tuskegee Institute, *Bulletin: Annual Report Edition of the Principal and Treasurer* (Tuskegee, 1911, 1914).

to Washington "three weaknesses . . . which have come about as a result of the progress which we are making." First, he noted, there was no real program for the training of teachers in spite of the term *normal* in the institute's name. Second, he asserted, Tuskegee was an industrial school, "but for the most part not a vocational school." Finally, he noted the stepchild status of the academic department, which had no independent training programs and failed to correlate its courses satisfactorily with the industrial departments. His major point was that the school lacked clearly defined programs of a true vocational nature. Students tended to receive bits of training from various departments, but the pieces did not fit together into a coherent whole to prepare a student for "one definite occupation." Although all of his proposals for the reorganization of courses and the granting of diplomas "of equal rank" from each department were not immediately implemented, Work was to influence the evolution of Tuskegee for the remainder of his years.[38]

Because he became a member of the extension department, which oversaw the school's outreach programs, Work also actively sought to improve their effectiveness. He was concerned that the work outside of Macon County was "very unsystematic and haphazard" and made suggestions regarding many extension activities. He recommended improvements in the local farmers' conferences, a different format for the annual Tuskegee Negro Farmers' Conference, and better training for extension workers. Work believed that extension work was probably the most significant aspect of Washington's program. He worked to expand the outreach of Tuskegee in numerous ways. For example, he played a prominent role in the establishment and continuation of National Negro Health Week.[39]

Clearly, in his role as record keeper and supplier of information for the institute, Work became a vital cog in the Tuskegee machine. When he decided to accept Washington's offer in 1908, Work fixed the direction of his career, for he had also to decide to forsake overt protest. His relationship with Du Bois was forever al-

38. Work to Washington, December 29, 1910, in Box 614, Washington to Work, March 7, 1910, in Box 604, both in Washington Papers.
39. Work to Washington, March 1, 1909, February 8, November 4, 1910, all in Box 604, Work to Washington, May 23, 1911, in Box 614, all *ibid.*

tered. The two men continued to work together on such projects as the Emancipation Proclamation Commission in 1913 and a proposed Encyclopedia of the Negro in the 1930s, and Du Bois made a conciliatory trip to Tuskegee in 1929, where he spoke to the Sociology Club. Nevertheless, Work's affiliation with the institute made them adversaries. There was friction between them over the Tuskegee Lynching Reports, for example, and over a review of the *Negro Year Book* in *Crisis*, the journal of the NAACP of which Du Bois was editor. Both men seemed to feel that the other was reluctant to share credit. Although relations between the NAACP and Tuskegee improved after Washington's death, DuBois still occasionally criticized the conservatism of Tuskegeans—including Monroe Work.[40]

Work managed for the most part, however, to avoid becoming a compromised man. With his faith in the impact of fact and his uncharismatic demeanor, Work's quiet, scholarly presentations were in keeping not only with Tuskegee's program but also with his own personality. In his role as loving critic, he was able to shape Tuskegee as much as he was shaped by it. Some scholars have noted that Washington became more outspoken on social issues in his later years. Although changing circumstances played a major role, the kind of information the principal received from Work was undoubtedly a factor. Work not only supplied him with the needed ammunition for a more aggressive battle, he also encouraged the principal's subtle shift from strict accommodationism. Indeed, throughout his almost forty years at Tuskegee, Monroe Work's was a quiet but insistent voice for change in the institute's approach to both education and race relations. As his seniority increased, all three Tuskegee presidents under whom he served relied more and more upon him in their attempts to update and revise the Tuskegee program. Of more importance, however, was his ability to expand his limited job description to establish a significant research program. His efforts helped to make Tuskegee Institute more truly "the center of things relating to the Negro."

40. Work to Scott, August 2, 1913, in Box 639, *ibid.*; Tuskegee *Messenger*, July, August, September, 1936, December 15–29, 1928, February 23, 1929; Work to Du Bois, January 25, 1932, copy enclosed in Work to Moton, January 28, 1932, in Box LC66, Moton Papers.

IV / The Research Would Allow
for Other Things

Other people were confused as to why he came to Tuskegee, but Monroe Work had few doubts. Although he intended to fulfill the requirements of his limited job description, he had always envisioned a much larger task for himself. As he later stated:

> When I came to Tuskegee, Educators and others seeking to advance the interest of the Negro were confronted with such questions as: What has the Negro accomplished? What can he do? Does it pay to educate him? Morally and physically, is he not deteriorating? Has his emancipation been justified? The publication, by Hoffman in 1896 of "Race Traits and Tendencies of the Negro," presented a more or less hopeless view. To the indictment of this publication there was at hand no effective answer. From 1908 on I was compiling a day by day record of what was taking place with reference to the Negro. Thus it became possible to answer in a factual manner questions relating to all matters concerning him.[1]

Of course, Work had not been hired to establish such a program, but from the beginning he realized the dual nature of his job. Thus, he suggested the title of Department of Records and Research, because "the Research would allow for other things." Throughout his career at Tuskegee, he exploited every possible opportunity to expand the scope and distribution of his "day by day record," and Washington's need for reliable data for his speeches and articles provided Work with the rationale for compiling an extensive body of material that could be put to other uses.

As early as December, 1908, Work submitted his "Plan for Mak-

---

1. Monroe N. Work, "An Autobiographical Sketch" (MS, February 7, 1940, in Box 1, Monroe Nathan Work Papers, Tuskegee Institute Archives).

ing Tuskegee a Greater Center for Information Relating to the Negro." The five-point plan specified the cataloging of current Tuskegee materials on Afro-Americans, the building of a select library of publications relating to blacks, the systematic gathering of data on the past and present conditions of blacks, the pursuit of research projects relating to Tuskegee and the Negro, and the production of a bibliography of publications on Afro-Americans.[2]

The largest jobs on this list were also the two that Work considered the most important: the systematic compilation of data and the production of a bibliography. These projects seemed crucial to him, for he believed that as a new and expanding field sociology should first be concerned with the accumulation of a "body of scientific facts" in order to become an "active, vital force in building and directing human relationships." Work's belief in the interrelatedness of the various social relationships convinced him that "investigations and researches should not be isolated, limited, unconnected, but should be conducted along broad and related lines covering every phase of association." If this were not done, he held, sociology would become too immediately practical, trying to understand and change one phase of society without realizing the effects the change might have on all other aspects of social life.[3]

According to Work, an accurate body of information would help to dispel misconceptions held by both blacks and whites. He was distressed that "like many white southern persons, we feel we know all about the Negro," and he claimed that this attitude prevented the systematic study of the Afro-American heritage and condition by blacks. It seemed to him that most blacks either accepted white stereotypes or refuted them blindly without adequate knowledge. "Our interest in acquiring information about ourselves," he stated, "is too much on the religious revival type, that is to say, it is too emotional."[4]

In 1908 there was certainly a need for the systematic collection

2. Monroe N. Work, "Plan for Making Tuskegee a Greater Center for Information Relating to the Negro" (MS, December 12, 1908, in Box 2, Work Papers).

3. Monroe N. Work, "Sociology in the Common Schools," *Proceedings of the American Sociological Society*, XIII (December, 1918), 95–97.

4. Tuskegee *Messenger*, April–May, 1935.

of data relating to all phases of the black experience. Except for discussions of the "race problem," white scholars virtually ignored the subject, and the number of trained black scholars was still very small. Although the few black scholars were making distinct contributions in specialized fields, only Atlanta University had a large-scale research program. The program was limited in scope, however, and it soon declined after Du Bois' departure in 1910. The American Negro Academy, established in 1897, was the only other major organization dedicated to black scholarship. It sponsored conferences and published occasional papers by its elected members, but Work envisioned a much more broadly based approach. In 1914 he and George E. Haynes of Fisk University attempted to organize a society of black researchers. Although their efforts failed, Carter G. Woodson succeeded the following year. He founded the Association for the Study of Negro Life and History, in which Work became an early participant, publishing an article in the first volume of the association's *Journal of Negro History*. Later Work also became a member of the ANA and supported the efforts of various groups that encouraged black studies. His own approach, however, remained unique. He undertook by himself the herculean task of systematically acquiring and organizing all kinds of information about blacks from every source.[5]

In an effort to provide a body of information with which to understand and change the position of blacks in American society, Work collected documents, books, pamphlets, articles, statistical data, press clippings, reports of various studies, and other material reflecting public opinion. His information came from a wide variety of sources. By 1922 more than 130 newspapers and periodicals—domestic and foreign, white and black—were handled weekly in his department. Other sources included material from three press clipping bureaus, books on the Negro, governmental reports, reports of special boards and commissions, and questionnaires on particular topics. As the department's reputation grew, individuals and agencies began to submit materials without being asked.[6]

5. Alfred A. Moss, Jr., *The American Negro Academy: Voice of the Talented Tenth* (Baton Rouge, 1981), 193–94.
6. Monroe N. Work, "Using a Collection of Materials on the Negro" (Type-

As information was obtained, it was classified into one of ninety-eight categories and filed alphabetically by year. This system allowed the easy retrieval of specific data for a given year. One had only to consult the appropriate category, such as agriculture, secret societies, or Jim Crow car laws. The collection grew to fill over thirty filing cabinets and served as the basis for replies to inquiries coming to Tuskegee. As it became more and more obvious that the department could be relied upon to furnish accurate information, Tuskegee's prestige grew. By 1916 Work could report that among those using the research materials of the department were the United States Bureau of Education, the United States Census Bureau, the Bureau of Research of the NAACP, and the Universities of Chicago, Pennsylvania, Wisconsin, Missouri, Virginia, and California.[7]

Because of the increasing demands for such information, Work was gradually able to alter the essential nature of his division, as his written reports on its activities show. At first most of Work's time was spent in compiling student records and in related endeavors; later his roles as publicist and source of data for the articles and speeches of others came to predominate. When the metamorphosis was completed, during Robert R. Moton's tenure as principal (1916–1935), the Department of Records and Research emerged as primarily a research center; many of its original duties had been absorbed by other people and divisions.

Although the transition was gradual, a major step was taken with the publication of the *Negro Year Book*, which began and developed almost by accident. In 1904 Andrew Carnegie established and funded the Committee of Twelve to disseminate publicity re-

---

script of address given at Fisk University, November 11, 1930, in Box 4, Work Papers); "Work Done in the Department of Records and Research of the Tuskegee Normal and Industrial Institute for the Year 1922–23" (Typescript in "Researches Being Made, 1922," Department of Records and Research Files, Tuskegee Institute Archives).

7. Monroe Work to Robert R. Moton, April 8, 1916, in Box LC5, Work to James R. Angell, December 4, 1920, in Box LC22, both in Robert Russa Moton Papers, Tuskegee Institute Archives. This material is still available in the Tuskegee Institute Archives for the years 1899 to 1966. Much of it has also been microfilmed by the National Historical Publications and Records Commission.

lating to the Negro. Washington and his fellow committee members used most of the money to publish and distribute pamphlets. By the summer of 1910, only a thousand dollars remained, and the principal thought of the materials Work had collected and his desire to publish them. In July he wrote Work about the possibility of compiling a yearbook of Negro progress to mark the fiftieth anniversary of emancipation in 1913.[8]

Washington envisioned the one-time publication of a pamphlet-size document, but Work quickly realized the potential of this opportunity. He suggested that the thousand dollars be used instead to publish a book of salable quality. The proceeds of its sale would replenish the fund, providing money for future projects. To that end, Dr. Robert E. Park, who was then in the sociology department of the University of Chicago, was consulted, and the Negro Year Book Publishing Company was formed.[9]

Under the terms of the agreement establishing the company, the *Negro Year Book* was to be edited by Work and jointly owned by Work, Park, and the Tuskegee Institute. Because the original funding would be provided by Washington and school time would be used in its preparation, the book could not be separated from Tuskegee. In addition to editing the yearbook, Work was to be responsible for its distribution; for these duties he was to receive two cents royalty on every copy sold. Park would handle the printing, publishing, and advertising, and Emmett J. Scott was to oversee the finances.[10]

The first edition, covering the year 1912, contained 225 pages and sold for twenty-five cents. It was at once a permanent record of current events, an encyclopedia of historical and sociological facts, a directory of persons and organizations, and a bibliographical guide to the subjects discussed. Only five thousand copies were printed, and they sold rapidly, providing funds for a 1913 edition. In

8. Monroe N. Work, interview by Lewis A. Jones, May 15, 1932 (Transcript in Box 1, Jessie P. Guzman Papers, Tuskegee Institute Archives); Booker T. Washington to Work, July 1, 1910, in Box 604, Booker T. Washington Papers, Library of Congress.

9. Work to Washington, July 5, 1910, in Box 604, Washington Papers.

10. "Agreement Between Emmett J. Scott, Robert E. Park, and Monroe Work Touching on the Negro Year Book" (Typescript, n.d., in Box 653, Washington Papers).

fact, the *Negro Year Book* was such a success that by the 1914–1915 edition its size had doubled and the number of copies printed had tripled. The company remained self-supporting through four editions, and then encountered financial difficulties in the distribution of the 1918–1919 edition. In 1928 it became necessary for Tuskegee Institute to assume the ownership of the *Negro Year Book* and pay its back debts. Nevertheless, eleven editions appeared between 1912 and 1952.[11]

Despite its haphazard beginning and shaky financial condition, the *Negro Year Book* was a remarkable publication. It made part of the files of the Department of Records and Research readily available to both professional and amateur scholars of the Afro-American experience. As the reputation of the *Negro Year Book* grew, scholars and other individuals began sending Work unsolicited information on unpublicized activities of individuals and organizations. They provided Work with a great deal of data that would have been difficult, if not impossible, to obtain otherwise. Every edition of the yearbook was so painstakingly verified and documented that cash prizes were offered for the discovery of a factual error. Each yearbook was a concise and reliable summary of the progress and setbacks of black people.[12]

While the *Negro Year Book* was, and still is, a valuable asset to the historian and sociologist, its impact was also significant among laymen. The facts it supplied inspired blacks with confidence in their ability to progress and refuted the rumors of black decline that were widespread among whites. The prestige of Tuskegee Institute lent credence to the facts presented in the yearbooks and allowed them to be distributed through white newspapers and to be accepted in both the North and South. Many southern editors published portions of the *Negro Year Book*, and such papers as the Houston *Post*, the Atlanta *Georgian*, the Charlotte *Observer*, and the Louisville *Review and Expositor* recommended it as both reliable and worthwhile. Upon reading the 1913 edition of the *Negro*

11. Monroe N. Work (ed.), *Negro Year Book, 1912* (Tuskegee, 1913); Moton, form letter, April 10, 1924, in Box LC33, Secretary of Board of Trustees to Work, May 1, 1928, in Box LC48, both in Moton Papers.

12. Tuskegee *Student*, November 28, September 2, 1916.

Year Book, one white editor was moved to write, "If those who believed as Carlyle did, that the black man would always need a master, could have foreseen the publication in 1914 of such figures as the *Negro Year Book* contains, all but the most stubborn would have been convinced." The *Republic* declared "The social, legal, financial, educational contrasts between the American Negro in 1863 and 1913 are by the very dispassion of their telling made miraculous. The book is written for reference use, yet many successive pages read like romance."[13]

Another valuable outcome of the publication of the *Negro Year Book* was its use in white schools for studies of the black experience. Several northern and southern public high schools ordered copies, and it was one of the texts recommended for Catholic schools. In addition, the Conference on Education and Race Relations, headquartered in Atlanta, furnished copies to selected high schools throughout the South.[14]

The enthusiastic reception of the first edition had still another very important effect: it provided concrete evidence of the value of the material Work had been accumulating. From his first days at Tuskegee, he had been proposing the expansion of his limited research duties, but the need for additional funding had barred the way. By 1912, however, the school was persuaded by the cumulative impact of the demand for Work's data, the issuance of semiannual lynching reports, and the preparation of the first *Negro Year Book* to seek money from Andrew Carnegie for a real research center at Tuskegee.[15]

Although these efforts were unfruitful, by the time of Booker T. Washington's death in November, 1915, the research component of Work's division had indeed grown in importance. The principal's death created an atmosphere of flux and change as a new principal was sought and found in the person of Robert Russa Moton of

13. Robert R. Moton to James R. Angell, November 17, 1920, in Box LC22, Moton Papers; Syracuse *Post Standard*, December 21, 1914; *Republic*, September 12, 1913 (Clippings in Box 5, Work Papers.)
14. Tuskegee *Messenger*, April–May, 1935.
15. Robert E. Park to James Bertram, February 13, 1912, in Box 18, Washington Papers.

Hampton Institute. Work realized that this was an appropriate time for another attempt to have the official status of his activities revised, and he wrote the acting principal, Warren Logan: "In view of the adjustments that are being made, I herewith request that the Division of Records and Research be made a Department of the Institution. The work which I instituted on coming here has after eight years of effort acquired enough reputation and importance throughout this county and elsewhere to be designated as a regular research department."[16]

His bid was initially unsuccessful, but in 1919 Work's efforts finally succeeded. In that year department status was granted and Work was made a member of the executive council. In addition, another request was made to the Carnegie Corporation, which finally bore fruit in 1921. A grant of approximately $8,500 a year for five years made it possible for Work to complete a long-term project he had started at Savannah—a comprehensive bibliography on the Negro in the United States. Over the next five years, Work and his staff collected more than thirty thousand references to produce a classified list of some ten thousand references. Negotiations were begun to have it published, but several events intervened to produce a more extensive bibliography.[17]

During the 1926 Founder's Day Week at Tuskegee, Anson Phelps-Stokes, a philanthropist and director of the Phelps-Stokes Fund, chanced to see the bibliography and became interested in it. He believed that Work should not limit the bibliography to the United States but should expand his material on Africa and include it as well. Work took the suggestion and added some three thousand references on Africa to his bibliography. Phelps-Stokes asked W. A. Slade, chief bibliographer of the Library of Congress, to examine the manuscript and suggest improvements. Arrangements were made to have the bibliography published by the H. W. Wilson Company. Then C. T. Loram, commissioner of native affairs for the Union of South Africa, visited Tuskegee Institute in the autumn of 1926 and looked over the manuscript. He suggested further expan-

16. Work to Warren Logan, April 8, 1916, in Box LC5, Moton Papers.
17. Monroe N. Work, "Making a Bibliography" (Typescript, n.d., in Box 1, Work Papers).

sion of the listings on Africa and recommended that Work send the bibliography to European scholars for their comments and help. Phelps-Stokes realized that more could be accomplished, and more quickly, if Work went directly to these men, and he offered to supply the needed money.[18]

Adequate funding was provided for a three-month trip with stops at London, Paris, The Hague, Brussels, Geneva, Hamburg, and Berlin. Florence Work would accompany her husband and aid his efforts as usual. After farewell fetes by the local temple of the Order of the Mystic Shrine and the Sociology Club, the Works left for New York on January 31, 1927, with a "beautifully bound journal in which to keep a record of the trip"—a present from Work's office staff.[19]

The couple received courteous treatment from government officials and library staffs during their tour, and Work's project was noted in several foreign newspapers. One article, which appeared in the Brussels *L'Indépendance*, described "the intellectual movement which has recently thrown itself on the black American world." Indeed, the trip occurred at the height of what has been called the Harlem Renaissance. That outpouring of black artistic and literary productivity often focused on the African origins of Afro-Americans and thus increased the need, as the article noted, for the kind of factual information to which the bibliography would provide a key.[20]

By the time they returned on May 6, the Works had collected an additional eleven hundred references, including some especially valuable British material on the slave trade. The resulting manuscript was published in 1928 and contained seventeen thousand references in seventy-four classified chapters, with the black authors designated by an asterisk. *A Bibliography of the Negro in Africa and America* was sorely needed at the time, for no adequate bibliography existed. The two leading bibliographies—the Atlanta University Studies No. 10, *A Selected Bibliography of the Negro*, and the Library of Congress publication, *A Select List of References on*

18. *Ibid.*
19. Tuskegee *Messenger*, February 12, 1927.
20. *Ibid.*, May 14, April 9, 1927.

the Negro Question—contained fewer than two thousand unclassi-
fied references each. Consequently, leading scholars in the field of
black studies immediately recognized the value of Work's bibliography. Charles S. Johnson called it "the beginning point of new ex-
plorations into the field of Negro literature."[21]

Without the dedication of Monroe Work, the bibliography might
never have been published. The H. W. Wilson Company was un-
willing to assume financial responsibility for its publication, and
when the fourteen-hundred-dollar Phelps-Stokes grant proved inadequate to cover printing costs, Work made up the difference of
almost seven hundred dollars from his personal funds. He also immediately began work on an expansion of the bibliography.[22]

The Department of Records and Research continued its major
tasks, working to expand the bibliography, to publish new editions
of the *Negro Year Book*, to prepare semiannual lynching reports, to
promote National Negro Health Week, to answer inquiries from
outside sources, and to supply the new principal with the same
sorts of information Washington had received. In addition, Work
and his staff also undertook more specialized research projects, and
although he spent the bulk of his time providing others with valuable tools for their own scholastic endeavors, Work continued to
engage in personal research that formed the basis for about seventy
articles and numerous speeches.

Work's department also participated in joint ventures with other
individuals and agencies. One of the first of these was a study of
black migration during World War I. In response to expanding opportunities in war-related industries in the North, combined with
dismal conditions in the South, blacks began a mass exodus from
the land of cotton that was to continue for many decades. The significance of this migration was recognized early, and in 1917 the
Carnegie Corporation provided a grant to Emmett J. Scott to study
the phenomenon. Scott had left Tuskegee during the war to become a special assistant to the secretary of war, but he remained

21. Monroe N. Work, *A Bibliography of the Negro in Africa and America*
(New York, 1928), vii; Charles Johnson to Work, August 13, 1928, in Box 1, Work
Papers.
22. Work to Moton, February 27, 1930, in Box LC52, Moton Papers.

aware of Work's research skills and selected him to conduct investigations in Alabama, Georgia, and Florida. He chose Charles S. Johnson to investigate Mississippi and centers in Missouri, Illinois, Wisconsin, and Indiana and assigned the eastern centers to T. Thomas Fortune, the former editor of the New York *Age*. Work was also asked to "get up a statistical statement of the movement of the Negro population during the last 40 years" and to compile the information in his collection on "(a.) regions from which large numbers are leaving, (b.) attitudes of the whites and colored, (c.) disturbances, (d.) economic consequences." In 1920 Oxford University Press published the results of the research as Volume 16 of the Preliminary Economic Studies of the War, a series sponsored by the Carnegie Endowment for International Peace.[23]

Work and others used the data he collected during this project to demonstrate the evils of southern race relations in a way whites could understand. His findings indicated that the pull of economic opportunity in the North was supplemented by the push of humiliation arising from the racial discrimination practiced by the white South. Since the drain of cheap labor was viewed with alarm by many white southerners, this black migration provided an ideal basis for spotlighting the need for change in such areas as lynching, the low appropriations for black education, and other discriminatory practices. Work skillfully exploited the situation with numerous articles in the *South Atlantic Quarterly*, the *National Economic League Quarterly*, and other journals.[24]

In such forums he used statistical data to demonstrate both the economic importance of the black population to the South and the impact of discrimination in such areas as wages, health, and educational appropriations. Thus he set the stage for suggesting that improvement in these areas would be in the economic interest of the

23. Emmett J. Scott, *Negro Migration During the War* (New York, 1920), v; Emmett J. Scott to Work, September 11, 1917, in Box LC9, Moton Papers.

24. Monroe N. Work, "The South's Labor Problem," *South Atlantic Quarterly*, XIX (January, 1920), 1–8; Monroe N. Work, "Conditions and Problems After the War," *National Economic League Quarterly*, II (November, 1916), 141; Monroe N. Work, "Effects of the War on Southern Labor," *Southern Workman*, XLVII (August, 1918), 381–84; Monroe N. Work, "Negro Migration in 1916–1917," *Southern Workman*, XLVII (November, 1919), 614–15.

South. Above all, he stressed that his migration studies showed that most "are not leaving because of wages, but they are going because they wish to be where they will be surer of better treatment" and that "one of the chief complaints of Negro labor . . . is against the indiscriminate use of the pistol by too many representatives of the law." The harsh treatment by law enforcement officials was of far more concern than lynching, according to Work, because "lynchings are more or less sporadic, [but] persecution and mistreatment by representatives of the law are something that Negro labor has continually to undergo." Work was especially interested in improving conditions in the South because he foresaw that blacks would face many problems in northern cities after the war—such as race riots growing out of competition for housing and jobs.[25]

Monroe Work's use of the migration study as a springboard for discussing the treatment of blacks in the South is a good example of the direction his protest proclivities followed while he was at Tuskegee. Relying heavily on statistical data and avoiding rhetorical excesses, he carefully exploited the opportunities provided by his Tuskegee connection to present persuasive cases for black progress and to combat the obstacles racism erected to that progress. His facts became potent weapons in the black struggle for equal rights.

After 1920 large-scale research projects became more common in the Department of Records and Research and indicated its changing nature. As the research component expanded, so did the staff and funding. Work had begun without even a full-time stenographer and as late as 1920 was assisted by only one clerk and one stenographer. After the receipt of the Carnegie grant in 1921, the staff rapidly increased; by 1925 it included two research assistants, two filing clerks, and two stenographers. By that time, so many journals and newspapers were being received that a full-time employee was added to the staff just to handle the mechanics of clipping and filing pertinent articles.[26]

25. Monroe N. Work, "Negro Migration," *Southern Workman*, LIII (May, 1924), 208; Monroe N. Work, "Cooperation and the South's New Economic Condition" (Typescript, n.d., in Box 3, Work Papers).

26. Jessie P. Guzman, my interview, January 6, 1982. The expansion of the department's staff and activities is evident from examining school bulletins and the principal's annual reports.

During this staff expansion, two individuals were hired who would play significant roles in the development of the department. The first was Ralph N. Davis, who received a B.A. degree in 1918 from Fisk University and that same year joined Tuskegee as the assistant to the director of extension. This position undoubtedly brought Davis into contact with Work, who hired him as a research assistant in 1920. Three years later, Jessie Parkhurst joined the staff. She was a member of a Savannah family that had long been close to Florence Work's family. After graduating from college, she lived in Montclair, New Jersey. When Work was on a trip to New York, she visited him. At that time he asked her to join his staff. Eventually, both Davis and Parkhurst (later Jessie P. Guzman) would head Work's department after his retirement.[27]

One of the first major projects following the Carnegie grant was a study by Work entitled "Changes in Population and Farm Tenure in Counties of the South by Color, 1880–1920." By 1923 statistics had been gathered from 535 counties in Alabama, Arkansas, Florida, Georgia, Kentucky, and Louisiana. This study was continued and expanded for many years, and the results were published by Work in several journal articles. Concurrently with that study, in the early 1920s the department also conducted a survey to determine "what studies relating to the Negro were being made in colleges, universities and elsewhere." At the same time, the department investigated the question, "What can the schools do to assist in increasing the efficiency of Negroes in trades and industries?"[28]

When the Carnegie grant expired in 1926, Work feared that the scope of his department's activities would have to be reduced. The staff was trimmed to four as the first belt-tightening measure. Then, that summer he was able to obtain a new grant from the Laura Spelman Memorial Fund, although it provided only four thousand dollars annually for three years. The following year Ralph Davis was granted a fellowship from the same fund to pursue graduate work at Columbia University in statistics and sociology.[29]

27. Ralph N. Davis, Vita (Typescript, n.d., in Box 2, Work Papers); Work to Logan, October 1, 1923, in Box LC33, Moton Papers; Guzman interview.

28. "Work of the Department of Records and Research for the Year 1922–1923," enclosed in Work to Moton, June 14, 1923, in Box LC38, Moton Papers.

29. Work to Moton, July 18, 1931, in Box LC33, May 31, 1926, in Box LC43,

A few years later Monroe Work received a grant of his own. The Rosenwald Fund provided money to finance his return to University of Chicago from October, 1931, to June, 1932. There he pursued postgraduate studies and continued his research in population changes and land tenure in the South. While the department's employees were improving their professional credentials, Tuskegee Institute was in the midst of its transition to college-level work. By the early 1930s both Parkhurst and Davis had begun to teach courses in sociology, thus further expanding the department's responsibilities.[30]

As the Great Depression deepened, the Tuskegee Institute, like schools throughout the country, was faced with acute financial problems. The administration moved to cut all nonessential expenditures, and Work's department naturally suffered from these cuts. Its major activities and new projects continued after the expiration of the Spelman grant only because Work was able to obtain outside funding once again. Beginning in 1930, the General Education Board, a Rockefeller philanthropic fund, provided six thousand dollars annually for five years. Without Work's skill at fund raising, the department might not have expanded, or even survived. As he noted in 1931, 63.5 percent of its total expenditures of $105,171.09 over the preceding ten years had come from special grants.[31]

The conditions arising from the Depression also had an impact on the department's research focus. This was natural enough, since almost all Americans were seeking to understand and to solve the problems created by the most severe economic collapse the nation had ever suffered. Although the beginning of the Depression is generally dated from the stock market crash in late 1929, farmers and some other segments of the economy had begun to feel the effects of the faltering economy years earlier. Even before the crash, President Herbert Hoover had addressed the problems of the farmers, albeit in the same timid, cautious manner that characterized his en-

---

both in Moton Papers; Work to Will W. Alexander, November 29, 1927, in Box 2, Work Papers.

30. Work to Moton, November 13, 1930, in Box LC52, September 19, 1931, in Box LC55, both in Moton Papers; Guzman interview.

31. Work to Moton, July 18, 1931, in Box LC33, Moton Papers.

tire approach to the great suffering growing from the economic failure. His agricultural program was administered by a federally sponsored farm board, which used a revolving fund of $500 million to make loans to national marketing cooperatives and to establish corporations to buy surpluses and thus raise prices. It was to become all too painfully typical of both Hoover's and Franklin D. Roosevelt's programs that little consideration was given to the impact on blacks. Although neither president deliberately discriminated against blacks, their solutions often reflected an ignorance of and insensitivity to the special conditions faced by Afro-Americans. This was especially tragic because blacks, who were stuck on the bottom rungs of the economic ladder, suffered more than any other group from the general decline. During the Depression black unemployment rates were generally twice as high as white ones.

By 1929 Monroe Work had accumulated enough data to be neither ignorant nor insensitive to the unique needs of blacks. During the discussions that preceded the passage of Hoover's Agricultural Marketing Act in 1929, Work became concerned that the legislation would not benefit black farmers as much as their white counterparts. He pointed out its shortcomings to Moton in the hope that he could use his influence to lobby for a better act.[32]

When it was passed, the act did little to relieve the plight of either black or white farmers, and this was a factor in Hoover's defeat in 1932, but his successor shared Hoover's ignorance of the special needs of blacks. Moreover, Roosevelt was limited by his dependence upon the southern congressional vote to enact his policies. The attitudes of Eleanor Roosevelt and such officials as Harold Ickes, the secretary of the interior, gave blacks some hope that their voices would be heard, however, and the new president did seem to be less insensitive than his predecessor. Even so, his earliest recovery legislation, the Agricultural Adjustment Act and the National Industrial Recovery Act, ignored the likely impact on blacks.

Naturally, black leaders and concerned whites sought to educate Roosevelt on the shortcomings of his programs in regard to Afro-

32. Work to Moton, April 19, 1929, in Box LC48, *ibid.*

Americans. As early as September, 1933, Monroe Work was corresponding with Will W. Alexander, a white leader of the Commission on Interracial Cooperation in Atlanta who was later appointed by Roosevelt to head the Farm Security Administration. Alexander wrote Work, "The more I study the situation in Washington, the more I am convinced that the government is pretty generally dependent on voluntary and unofficial agencies for information to deal intelligently with local situations far removed from Washington."[33]

This recognition led to a collaborative venture by the CIC and Tuskegee Institute to supply the needed data on the impact of New Deal programs on blacks. At first Work focused on the enforcement of the National Recovery Administration's codes regulating wages and working conditions. The agency had been established to promote recovery in the industrial sector; two of the evils it sought to remedy were the massive wage cuts and layoffs that were escalating the downard spiral of the economy. But the NRA's impact on black joblessness and low pay was minimized from the outset, first, because there were relatively few blacks in industrial jobs and, second, because it provided for regional differences in prescribed wage scales, allowing lower wages to be paid in the South. It was crucial to ensure that blacks were not further discriminated against in the enforcement of the various codes. Since the federal government was not closely monitoring local situations, Work launched an investigation of the NRA in Alabama. Ralph Davis studied conditions in Birmingham, Mobile, and Montgomery from October to December, 1933.[34]

From interviews with both employers and employees, Davis quickly learned that some of the larger industries—often those that were part of national conglomerates—were complying with NRA codes in a nondiscriminatory manner, and some blacks were enjoying reduced hours and increased pay. Nevertheless, the overall

33. Alexander to Work, September 27, 1933 (Copy in "Negro and the N.R.A. in the State of Alabama, 1933," Records and Research Files).

34. Ralph M. Davis, "Survey in Alabama, October 27 to November 8 and December 4 to 9, of the Office of the Operation of the N.R.A. Code on Negro Labor" (Typescript, n.d., in "Negro and the N.R.A. in the State of Alabama, 1933," Records and Research Files).

effect of the codes on black workers was harmful. At worst, blacks lost their jobs; they were frequently dismissed and replaced with white labor when the mandated wage increases made their jobs more attractive to whites. Sometimes they were paid lower wages than whites for identical work, often on the basis of management claims that black labor was less efficient than white. Employers used numerous loopholes to technically comply with the law without actually meeting wage and hour standards. Sometimes job descriptions were changed; one black porter was labeled and paid as a bootblack while continuing to do the work of a porter. Raises were given and then taken away in the form of deductions for such things as waitresses' uniforms and delivery boys' bicycles. Some salaried employees were put on commission; others were asked to work longer hours than were reported. Often employees were threatened with dismissal if they publicly complained.[35]

The CIC support of the study ensured the cooperation of black and white scholars throughout the state. Among the whites, none was more active than J. R. Steelman at Alabama College in Montevallo. He not only verified Davis' findings but was also privy to information unavailable to blacks. For example, he reported one county director of a federal work relief program as saying, "We will not give jobs to Negroes while white men need them." The results of the study were sent to various New Deal officials and presented to the Emergency Advisory Council for Negroes.

Although the NRA was scrapped when its codes were declared unconstitutional, the initial study provided concrete evidence of discrimination in the local administration of New Deal programs. Thus, the CIC decided to expand the scope of the investigation and increase its funding to Tuskegee and other agencies. Discrimination was never totally eliminated from the New Deal, but the evidence collected by Work and others forced some attempts to remedy the situation, including the appointment of Alexander to the Farm Security Administration. The study and its consequences undoubtedly reinforced Work's faith in the "impact of fact."[36]

35. *Ibid.*
36. J. R. Steelman to Work, November 9, 20, 1933, Arthur Raper to Work, February 20, 1934, both in "Negro and the N.R.A. in the State of Alabama,

The declining economic opportunities for blacks during the Great Depression also led the Department of Records and Research to conduct a study, "Trends and Tendencies in the Occupations of Negroes." Beginning in 1935, the study was funded by the General Education Board and was intended to supply blacks with useful information on which to base career choices. Shortly after it began, the Department of Labor launched a similar study, and Work suggested a cooperative effort to promote the sharing of information and to prevent the duplication of efforts.[37]

These two projects consumed much of the department's resources during the 1930s, but smaller-scale projects were also undertaken by various members of the department, studies such as "Settlers in Counties in Alabama," "Public Opinion and the Negro Woman," and "The Role of the Negro Newspaper in Negro Life." In addition, at Work's suggestion the department took possession of the personal and professional papers of Booker T. Washington. Work was responsible not only for the preservation of these valuable documents but also for their donation to the Library of Congress, where they have been used by numerous scholars.[38]

By the time of Work's retirement in 1938, the functions of his department had greatly expanded. It had come to encompass a unique blend of roles, many of which would later be assumed by a variety of people and departments at Tuskegee. In the course of Work's tenure, the Department of Records and Research had functioned as a placement bureau, a public relations office, a social science research center, an academic department, an archive, and an extension bureau. Fortunately for later scholars, Work's persistence in developing the research component of his department succeeded. Much of the department's own research was significant, and many scholars have benefited from its files, the *Negro Year Book, A Bibliography of the Negro in Africa and America*, and the collection of Washington's papers—all are part of Monroe Work's priceless legacy to scholarship.

1933," Records and Research Files; Work to Moton, January 27, 1934, in Box LC65, Moton Papers; Tuskegee *Messenger*, August, 1934.

37. Work to Lawrence A. Oxley, July 10, 1935, Oxley to Work, August 21, 1935, both in Box 2, Work Papers.

38. Work to F. D. Patterson, March 18, 1943, in Box 2, Work Papers.

V / Negroes Should Not Despise the Rock from Which They Were Hewn

As director of the Department of Records and Research at Tuskegee Institute, Monroe Work was a systematic and painstaking compiler of data on the black experience. Yet his quiet, scholarly demeanor belied the deep, driving passion that motivated and guided him both as a man and as a sociologist. From his speeches and articles a clearer picture of his philosophical frame of reference emerges. Through all his writings and lectures, there is one connecting thread—his conviction that both blacks and whites were crippled by popular, erroneous conceptions of black inferiority. He fully realized the role of earlier scholars in forming shallow, inaccurate racial stereotypes and once noted:

> When I was a small boy in school I was greatly interested in reading in geographies and other books about the five races of mankind. I found much to admire and wonder about in the descriptions and pictures of all of these races excepting the black, or Negro. For this one I always had a sort of pity and a feeling that his picture was put in the geography because he could not well be omitted and that it served as a sort of contrast to emphasize the superiorities of the other races. Later in university classes on anthropology and ethnology I learned why the Negro was made to appear to be such a bad looking creature. . . . I found that the nature and value of the type depends on who makes it and the purpose for which it is made. Types which are created or chosen by the people that they are to represent are generally idealistic, that is, they set forth the best features of the people. . . . On the other hand types which are created by persons outside of the race for purposes of ridicule and disparagement usually set forth the ridiculous, the absurd, the uncouth and whatever will tend to show forth the weaknesses of the race.[1]

1. Monroe N. Work, "An Anthropological Study of Negro Types," National Baptist Union *Review*, November 19, 1910, as reprinted in Tuskegee *Student*, January 14, 1911.

White scholarship had produced falsehoods; black scholarship had to reveal the truth. This was the task to which Monroe Work dedicated his life. His goal shaped both his scholarly, well-researched articles for professional journals and his more sermon-ish writings aimed at black audiences. Always he depicted blackness as both different and beautiful. He believed that blacks had made significant contributions to mankind and would continue to do so if the crippling stigmas arising from their color were removed. His articles and speeches covered a wide range of subjects, but all were directed toward either recording black progress or illuminating the obstacles to it.

The focus and nature of Work's scholarship reflected the conditions of his era. All people are influenced by current values and beliefs; by either accepting or rejecting the status quo, all are forced to respond to it. Those who seek change must couch their arguments in terms that their generation can understand and accept. This interaction between the individual and society is evident in Work's attempts to instill black pride and eradicate white prejudice. He did not openly challenge the yardstick by which human achievement was then measured; he merely questioned the accuracy of the measurements. From historical hindsight his approach does not seem revolutionary, but in the context of his time he was truly remarkable.

One way he differed from his contemporaries at the turn of the century was in his preoccupation with African history and culture. Most scholars then viewed Africa with a paternalism that implicitly recognized the present inferiority of the continent and ignored the existence of an African past.[2] For many white scholars, the "backwardness" of Africa in technology and political organization was proof of the inferiority of blacks. Europe and the United States were at the apex of their power, carving up most of the rest of the world into official empires or unofficial spheres of influence. To justify the naked exploitation of others, the concept of "Western

2. See August Meier, *Negro Thought in America, 1880–1915* (Ann Arbor, 1963); George Shepperson, "Notes on Negro American Influence on the Emergence of African Nationality," *Journal of African History*, I (1960), 299–312.

civilization" proved invaluable. By defining civilization in terms of European development—technological advances, the nation-state, individualism, and capitalism—it became possible to claim credit for "civilizing" the rest of the world. It was even more psychologically useful to believe that the benefits derived from this "civilization" had never been, and could never be, achieved without European help.

These subconscious assumptions shaped the writing of history. Western history became world history, since all good things that had ever happened to mankind obviously came from Europe and its offspring, the United States. The terms *Western* and *European* were expanded or contracted depending on the circumstances. Ancient Egyptians were European; modern ones were not. The fact that more than half of man's recorded history had passed before a single person on the European continent could read or write was conveniently ignored.

Most blacks, Monroe Work among them, were educated with books written by whites and based on their yardstick for measuring civilization. Thus, at the beginning of the twentieth century, black scholars tended to view Africa with a mixture of embarrassment and paternalism. As the largest group of "Europeanized" African descendants, they assumed it was their task to join with other westerners to civilize the continent. Booker T. Washington has been described as having "thoroughly subscribed to the 'White Man's Burden' of leadership and authority [so] that, in seeming forgetfulness that he was a Negro, he actively took up the burden himself."[3]

Although Work never overtly challenged the European definition of civilization, he did work to refute the notion that Africa had always been "backward" in terms of technology and political organization. Instead of viewing the African heritage as unworthy of attention, he became preoccupied with discovering the truth of the African past, especially after his contacts with William I. Thomas at Chicago. Although never able to fulfill his cherished dream of

3. Louis R. Harlan, "Booker T. Washington and the White Man's Burden," *American Historical Review*, LXXI (January, 1966), 442.

visiting Africa, Work read practically everything he could find relating to the continent, including European works and the earlier Arab sources. He began to realize that Africa was not without a history, even if there was no widespread tradition of written records.

Discovering aspects of African history that he had never encountered in his schoolbooks, Work disseminated his findings as widely as possible through articles and speeches. Soon after coming to Tuskegee, he was given a new forum when Washington asked him to present a series of yearly lectures on Africa to Tuskegee students. His well-organized lecture notes reflect the best available scholarship and present a picture, not of a savage people to be uplifted, but of a unique people with a sometimes glorious past. He described how the black kingdom of Ethiopia (Kush) had conquered the mighty Egypt in the eighth century B.C. He also told of the medieval kingdoms of the Sudan, which had often surpassed their European contemporaries in size, wealth, military strength, and influence. Ghana, Mali, and Songhai were described as great trading and cultural centers, which were in close contact with the Arab world. He shared Arab accounts of such African leaders as Mansa Musa, Sonni Ali, and Askia Mohammad, and such cultural centers as Timbuktu and Jenné. It must have surprised these students, who had heard only of cannibals and missionaries in their white-controlled elementary schools, to learn that the Europeans had not had a monopoly on power or scholarship.[4]

Work told of other great ancient African states but did not ignore the more recent history of Africa. He asserted that colonization, instead of civilizing the continent, had had a rather negative impact on Africa. The imposition of European laws and customs had, Work believed, "for almost 400 years . . . worked injury to the African." All good things had not come from Europe.[5]

Although keenly interested in African political and military history, Work's primary concern was the cultural heritage of Africa.

4. Monroe N. Work, "The Kingdom of the Sudan" (Typescript, n.d., in Box 8), "An Ancient Negroid Nation" (Typescript, n.d., in Box 7), both in Monroe Nathan Work Papers, Tuskegee Institute Archives.

5. Monroe N. Work, "The Partition of Africa" (Typescript, n.d., in Box 8, Work Papers).

Combining his sociological skills and a true love of Africa, he sought to present "the African in a dignified manner and not from the Uncle Remus standpoint." He was especially impressed with the Africans' early use of iron smelting, but he also discussed the boatbuilding, pottery-making and basket-weaving skills of African peoples. He enlightened Tuskegee students by informing them that cotton goods had once been exported from Africa to Portugal and that this pattern of trade had not been reversed until the late eighteenth century.[6]

Of course, this kind of information still measured African success by the European yardstick. In his earliest published articles on Africa, the European standard of civilization is even more evident. These first published essays were based on papers he had written at the University of Chicago and thus reflected William I. Thomas' strong influence on the young scholar. Although Thomas rejected many white stereotypes, he accepted the current belief that societies ranged from primitive to civilized. In his view, social groups progressed toward civilization, and all groups followed a similar course in this progress. Thus, Work's series entitled "Some Parallelisms in the Development of Africans and Other Races," which was published in the *Southern Workman* in 1906 and 1907, traced the evolution of different cultural aspects including language, economics, family structure, and sex role differentiation in Africa and compared them to those of other societies.[7]

In a later article it is apparent that Work had become more ambivalent about European notions of success. On the one hand, his primary emphasis was still the accomplishments of the early Africans in technology and politics. Evidently, he had also accepted European standards of beauty, for he quoted a German scholar who had written:

Open an illustrated geography and compare the "type of the African Negro," the bluish-black fellow of the protuberant lips, the flattened

6. Monroe Work to Carter G. Woodson, July 13, 1927, in Box 2, Monroe N. Work, "African Work in Iron" (Typescript, February, 1944, in Box 8), Monroe N. Work, "African Handicrafts" (Typescript, n.d., in Box 7), all in Work Papers.
7. Monroe N. Work, "Some Parallelisms in the Development of Africans and

nose, the stupid expression and the short curly hair, with the tall bronze figures from Dark Africa with which we have of late become familiar, their almost fine-cut features, slightly arched nose, long hair, etc., and you have an example of the problems pressing for solution. In other respects, too, the genuine African of the interior bears no resemblance to the accepted Negro type as it figures on drug and cigar store signs, wearing a shabby stovepipe hat, plaid trousers, and a vari-colored coat.

Nevertheless, in the same article Work asked why the Negro could not attain superiority along lines of his own and, "instead of simply patterning after what the white man has done, . . . through music, art, history, and science, make his own special contributions to the world." He also decried the fact that the black man "has come largely to believe in his inherent inferiority and that to attain superiority he must become like the white man in color, in achievements and, in fact, along all lines." Yet how difficult it was for Work to reject European standards of behavior can be clearly seen in the conclusion of the article.

> From this brief sketch which I have given of the African in ancient and medieval times it is clear that Negroes should not despise the rock from which they were hewn. As a race they have a past which is full of interest. It is worthy of serious study. From it we can draw inspiration; for it appears that not all black men everywhere throughout the ages have been "hewers of wood and drawers of water." On the contrary through long periods of time there were powerful black nations which have left the records of their achievements and of which we are just now beginning to learn a little. This little, however, which we have learned teaches us that the Negroes of today should work and strive. Along their own special line and in their own peculiar way they should endeavor to make contributions to civilization. Their achievements can be such that once more black will be dignified and the fame of Ethiopia again spread throughout the world.[8]

It is impossible to know to what extent Work realized the duality of his response to Africa. He was probably too much a creature

---

Other Races," *Southern Workman*, XXXV, XXXVI (November, 1906, January, February, March, 1907), 614–21, 37–43, 105–11, 166–75.

8. Monroe N. Work, "The Passing Tradition and African Civilization," *Journal of Negro History*, I (January, 1916), 34–41.

of his environment and training to consciously question the European world view. If he did, he was shrewd enough to know that a vision of civilization based on such factors as the quality of interpersonal relationships and the richness of artistic expression was culturally unacceptable at the time. To stress such themes was to seem to apologize for Africa's failure to excel in more recognized ways. The focus, if not the conclusions, of many of his articles indicates that Work at least unconsciously recognized that the real achievements of Africa were found in its culture, not its kingdoms. In this respect he was ahead of his time and even ahead of many later scholars, both black and white.

Work's interest in the African cultural and human heritage is evident in such studies as those of the African family and African agriculture. These articles were mainly descriptive; Work rarely made value judgments. Drawing from numerous eyewitness accounts, he presented a rich and complex tapestry of customs and beliefs. In this, he also differed from many scholars, then and later. He usually avoided the common error of describing Africa as a monolithic cultural unit and was careful to note Africa's diversity.[9]

Work's preoccupation with Africa was more than merely academic. He perceived much earlier than many scholars the importance of African survivals in current Afro-American culture, as can be seen in his longtime interest in black folk tales. He painstakingly collected versions of Afro-American and African folk tales and parables, often noting the similarities. Evidently, he did not view the African heritage as remote and distant, but as a living influence in the United States. Although he never clearly articulated a vision of the positive impact of African cultural survivals, he was obviously ahead of most of his black contemporaries, for he at least did not ignore or deny them.[10]

9. Monroe N. Work, "The African Family as an Institution," *Southern Workman*, XXXVIII (June, July, August, 1909), 343–53, 319–97, 433–40; Monroe N. Work, "The African Medicine Man," *Southern Workman*, XXXVI (October, 1907), 561–64; Monroe N. Work, "An African System of Writing," *Southern Workman*, XXXVII (October, 1908), 518–26; Monroe N. Work, "African Agriculture," *Southern Workman*, XXXIX (November, December, 1910), 613–18, and XL (January, February, 1911), 37–42, 79–87.

10. Monroe N. Work, "Some Geechee Folklore," *Southern Workman*, XXXIV

Work had become interested in Africa as a tool for understanding the Afro-American experience largely because of Thomas' assertion of the importance of social origins of groups. His sociological training, rooted in the social gospel, led him to emphasize present conditions in his studies of blacks in the United States. Work pursued knowledge not merely for its own sake but also to provide solutions to current problems. His ultimate goals were to instill black pride and to eradicate white prejudice. For blacks, increased self-esteem combined with a realistic appraisal of conditions could provide a basis for action. Whites, he hoped, would cease discriminatory practices if they were made aware of black ability and of the impact of unjust conditions arising from racism. Thus, in speeches and articles about black Americans, Work sought to highlight black achievement and to focus attention on the barriers to further advancement.

In "A Half Century of Progress," Work contrasted the status of blacks in 1866 and 1922 to illustrate black potential. In spite of the handicapping legacies of slavery and an environment of discrimination, in about fifty years blacks had increased literacy by 70 percent and had vastly improved their economic status. The number of homes owned by blacks had grown from 12,000 to 650,000 units and their accumulated wealth had expanded from $20 million to $1.5 billion. Reminding the readers that the black population of the United States was greater than the combined populations of Norway, Sweden, and Denmark, Work noted that no other emancipated people had made so much progress in so short a time. To illustrate his point, he contrasted the Russian serfs, emancipated in 1861, with the freedmen of the United States. He found that the serfs had advanced to only 30 percent literacy and an accumulated wealth of only about thirty-six dollars per capita, while black Americans had

---

(November, December, 1905), 633–34, 696–97; Monroe N. Work, "Folk Tales from Students in the Georgia State College," *Journal of American Folklore*, XXXII (July–September, 1919), 402–405; Monroe N. Work, "Folk Tales from Students in Tuskegee Institute, Alabama," *Journal of American Folklore*, XXXIV (July–September, 1919), 397–401. See also the lecture notes in Box 7, Work Papers.

reached an 80 percent literacy rate and a wealth of over a hundred dollars per capita.[11]

In a similar article Work asserted, "We are too prone to measure achievement in economic terms. There are other values—moral, spiritual and intellectual—to be taken into account. These are difficult to present in a factual manner, but some indirect evidence of such progress is indicated in the emphasis which, through the years, the group has placed on home building and the imparting of moral and spiritual precepts to the children in the home." He also frequently noted that "no other people have given a larger percentage of their earnings for religious work. Over eight percent of the total wealth of the Negroes is in church property."[12]

Returning to his native state in 1929, Work reiterated the theme of Negro progress before an American Historical Association meeting at Durham, North Carolina. "It is safe to say," he declared, "that any people starting out with a handicap of poverty and ignorance, who can in fifty years become owners of one-fourth of all the homes they now occupy, are making progress along those lines which make for a high degree of citizenship." To the predominantly white audience, he talked of barriers other than ignorance and poverty, especially the white primary. In the effort to reduce black political power at the turn of the century, southern whites had adopted measures that could skirt the provisions of the Fifteenth Amendment, which forbade denial of the vote on the basis of race, color, or previous condition of servitude. Some states had hit upon the method of barring blacks from voting in the Democratic primary on the premise that the Democratic party was a private organization, free to determine its own membership. Of course, in the one-party South, the Democratic primary was, to all intents and purposes, the election. Work asserted that this practice hurt whites as well as blacks by lowering the voter participation of both. In view of the voting results in states with disfranchisement laws,

11. Monroe N. Work, "A Half Century of Progress: The Negro in America in 1866 and 1922," *Missionary Review of the World*, XLV (June, 1922), 431, 440.

12. Monroe N. Work, "Two Generations Since Emancipation," *Missionary Review of the World*, LIX (June, 1936), 289–90.

Work asked "whether, in keeping the Negro in the political ditch, the Democratic party, in these states, has not been compelled to remain in the ditch with them."[13]

These were not mild words. Yet in this speech and others Work was able to present facts and opinions that might have been less acceptable from another source. His scholarly demeanor and his connection with the respected Tuskegee Institute fostered a certain amiability in white audiences, though Work often spoke of white unfairness in terms that were unmistakable. Yet his words were never tinged with bitterness perhaps because he was so remarkably sensitive to the complexities of race relations and especially to white public opinion. Work recognized a central problem of black Americans in the fact that to "the average person in this country, the term Negroes suggests a mass of black ignorant people all of whom occupy menial positions."[14] Although prejudice might not miraculously disappear when the facts were known, it certainly could not diminish so long as the popular misconceptions prevailed. Therefore, he believed it was essential to educate as well as agitate. He did not reject agitation, but left it to those more personally and professionally suited for it.

One way in which Work sought to educate the white public was to exploit any event that increased its receptiveness to his message. The emphasis on democratic ideals during World War I provided such an opportunity, and on numerous occasions Work spoke out for the extension of democracy at home. Realizing that vast changes would arise from the war and the peace process, in 1918 he asked two questions: "Will the Negro peoples of the world be able to attain that efficiency which will enable them to hold their own in the fierce struggle, commercial and industrial, that will take place following the coming of peace?" and "Will the principles of democracy be so applied to Negroes that they will be able to take part in this struggle on the same basis as other peoples?" Dur-

13. Monroe N. Work, "The Economic Progress of the Negro" (Typescript of the address to the American Historical Association in Durham, N.C., December 31, 1929, in Box 3, Work Papers).
14. Monroe N. Work, "The Negro and Public Opinion During the Period of the World War" (Typescript, n.d., in Box 3, Work Papers).

ing the same year, in a speech before a biracial group, Work declared the desire of black Americans, "while the Negro soldier from here is 'somewhere in France,' battling that the world may be made safe for democracy, that at the same time the South may be made safe for the most humble Negro who toils for his daily bread."[15]

Keenly aware of Afro-American health problems and black victimization by white lynch mobs, Work appealed to the economic interests of whites to persuade them to join with blacks to eradicate these menaces. Black migration during and after World War I made this kind of appeal especially relevant. The South was alarmed by its shrinking labor force and sometimes resorted to threatening blacks and requiring migration agents to pay a thousand-dollar license fee. In describing the situation Work said, "When the South saw her labor supply moving away, her attitude changed, the same Negroes who a short time before were spoken of as lazy, shiftless and as burdens to the South, were now said to be the best workers in the world."[16]

Although Work believed that migration might benefit blacks, he took advantage of the panic among whites to argue that the exodus of black labor from the South would halt only when the wages there were raised to equal those paid in the North. He also suggested that efforts be made to see that Negroes received just treatment and a fair deal in the South. He acknowledged the economic motivations behind the movement, but he pointed out some of the social conditions that aggravated the situation. These included lynching, discrimination in the application of the law, Jim Crow and disfranchisement laws, neglect of Negro residential areas and schools, and the insulting attitude and treatment blacks endured at the hands of whites. Work noted that the efficiency of the labor supply that still remained could be greatly improved by white efforts in the fields of black education and health.[17]

15. Monroe N. Work, "The Negro and Democracy," *Southern Workman*, XLVI (May, 1918), 219; Monroe N. Work, "Southern Labor as Affected by the War and Migration" (Typescript of address to the Southern Sociological Congress in Birmingham, Ala., April 15, 1918, in Box 3, Work Papers).

16. John Hope Franklin, *From Slavery to Freedom* (4th ed.; New York, 1974), 472; Work, "The Negro and Public Opinion."

17. Monroe N. Work, "The South's Labor Problem," *South Atlantic Quar-*

Work also tapped the reform spirit of the Progressive era in his fight for improved conditions for blacks. That wave of reform, which spanned the first two decades of the century and resulted in a plethora of legislation to remedy social ills, largely ignored the problems of black Americans. Noting the discussions about women's suffrage, Work described the impact of the Thirteenth, Fourteenth, and Fifteenth Amendments in a talk entitled "Would Gradual Emancipation Have Been Better for Negroes?" After explaining the provisions of each amendment and the proposed alternatives, he concluded:

> Until Emancipation and the adoption of the War Amendments, the application of the general principles of the Declaration of Independence and of the Constitution was confined to white men. What the war amendments did was to affirm that the Declaration of Independence and the Bill of Rights applied to all men, no matter what their color. Would gradual emancipation have brought about the same results? It is doubtful. As it is, the Emancipation Proclamation and the War Amendments are the Magna Charta of the colored races, not only in this country, but in every part of the world, wherever they have come under the domination of the white man's law. These Amendments are basis on which . . . the darker races everywhere are demanding that the principles of democracy be extended and applied to them on the same basis as they are extended and applied to white races.[18]

True to the Tuskegee ideals, Work always recognized the duality of black problems in America in the early twentieth century. Undoubtedly, black opportunity was unfairly limited by white repression. Yet it would be unrealistic not to admit that a large number of blacks, only a few generations away from crippling slavery, were not equipped to compete effectively even in a completely free and open society—especially one in such a rapid state of change. Filled with the moralistic ardor of a crusader, Work preached to his people of racial cooperation and black responsibility, exhorting them to

---

terly, XIX (January, 1920), 1–8; Work, "Southern Labor as Affected by War and Migration"; Monroe N. Work (ed.), Negro Year Book, 1918–1919 (Tuskegee, 1920), 12.

18. Monroe N. Work, "Would Gradual Emancipation Have Been Better for the Negroes?" (Typescript, n.d., in Box 3, Work Papers).

live up to their high potential and not to be sidetracked by such evils as whiskey.[19]

Subscribing to a modified view of Du Bois' theory of the Talented Tenth, Work sincerely believed that educated Negroes were obligated to help their fellow blacks. The Negro churches, he felt, needed to take a more active part in the social and economic betterment of their congregations. True to his belief in the social gospel, he declared that it was time for churches to stop being a haven of refuge; the churches should begin trying to redeem the world and make it a fit place in which to live. He argued that black teachers also had a duty to "teach men how to sacrifice for the good of the community." The competent teacher should possess "not only ability to do the classroom work well, but likewise ability to do work for the community's betterment."[20]

Work's ideas of self-help were clearly in line with the Tuskegee ideal of Booker T. Washington, but they should not be as simplistically interpreted as Washington's thinking has been. To assume that Work had a blind allegiance to the Protestant work ethic or a sense of black responsibility for the race's plight is a mistake. He believed, and freely asserted to whites, that the American doctrine of success through hard work had to be revised when applied to blacks. He declared that there were two categories of race problems. Blacks, he recognized, were hampered by their own backwardness and lack of progressivism, which led to economic inefficiency and exploitation, as in peonage. But the other category of race problem was generated by the very progressiveness of some Afro-Americans. As blacks moved up the social and economic scale, they encountered new infringements of their rights and privileges. For example, Work noted, so long as blacks were financially unable to purchase land in white neighborhoods, there had been little attempt to enact residential segregation laws. Only

19. Monroe N. Work, "The Negro's Industrial Problem," *Southern Workman*, XLIII (August–September, 1914), 428–39; Savannah *Tribune*, August 12, 1905.

20. Monroe N. Work, "The Negro Church and the Community," *Southern Workman*, XXXVII (August, 1908), 428–32; Monroe N. Work, "How to Fit the School to the Needs of the Community," *Southern Workman*, XXXVII (September, 1908), 505–506.

around 1910, after considerable black financial and social progress, did agitation arise in some cities for legally closed housing.[21]

Although Work was decidedly against legal or quasi-legal segregation, he, like many other blacks of the period, teetered somewhat ambiguously between racial solidarity and assimilation. In 1920 he implied that blacks would be happy to live in black neighborhoods under certain conditions.

> Why do[es the] Negro buy in a neighborhood where there are whites? The reason is simple. Only in white neighborhoods are there sanitary conditions. He wants to live on a street where there are lights. He wants to get out from the brothels and dives. He wants to get on a street where water connections offer him more protection from fire and cut down his insurance. . . . If the cities would give Negroes their proportionate part of municipal improvements in the way of pavements, sewers, lights, police protection, and so forth, they would do much more than they were doing by passing segregation laws.

Five years later, however, in drafting a letter for Robert Moton, Work explained that he had carefully avoided mentioning superior facilities as a motive for moving into white neighborhoods. He felt it might give the impression that, if provided equal accommodations, blacks "should be forced to live in neighborhoods which were set apart for them by the white people"—a belief that carried with it "the same idea of compulsion as in the case of the Jim Crow car law."[22]

The sense of conflict is also found in comparing Work's emphasis on the unique and significant contributions of the black cultural heritage with his desire for Negro assimilation or "absorption into the life, the spirit of the nation." At times it even appeared that he desired his fellow blacks to pattern their lives according to white mores and customs. For example, in 1910 he said: "We have all the wants and needs which are common to the other people of this country, and, in addition, we have an environment peculiarly our

21. Monroe N. Work, "The Progress of the American Negro in Property Holding and Its Significance for the Future of the Race" (Typescript of address to the Southern Sociological Congress in Washington, D.C., May 13, 1920, in Box 4, Work Papers).

22. *Ibid.*; Work to Robert R. Moton, October 6, 1925, in Box LC38, Robert Russa Moton Papers, Tuskegee Institute Archives.

own. Our especial effort must be to change this environment."[23] Taken in the context of Work's career and his other writings, however, these remarks clearly applied to opportunities, not mores and customs. He did not yearn for black to become white but only for American society to accept in its culture both that which was black and that which was white.

In fact, Work quite often praised the inner qualities that he felt were typical of blackness. He spoke of the cheerfulness of blacks, who would seldom let their burdens drag them down, and of their perseverance in the struggle for a better life despite limitations, stating that "black women literally through the washtub have helped to educate the race." Most important to Work was the black spirit which found its highest expression in "not trying to prevent another from having the opportunity to have and enjoy all the privileges and rights of a free and full life." The efforts of blacks to help one another were especially significant to him, and he often wrote articles on cooperative efforts in black communities and self-help organizations.[24]

Work was also proud of black literary achievements, but he believed that the personal, subjective poetry of the slaves was superior to the impersonal, objective dialect poetry of his era. The more recent poetry, he asserted in 1908, described only the "mere externalities" of black existence; it "amuses but does not ennoble or inspire." To the Negro poet, Work issued a call to voice the "hopes, longings, and aspirations" of black people and to "sing of their sorrows." Then, he said, the poet would become "the mouthpiece of the people and express what they but dumbly feel."[25]

While recognizing the beauties in the black experience, Work

23. Monroe N. Work, "The Importance of Exact Race Knowledge" (Typescript of address to the All Races Conference in Chicago, Ill., February 13, 1924, in Box 4, Work Papers); Monroe N. Work, "Problems of Education," *Southern Workman*, XXXIX (October, 1910), 521.

24. Monroe N. Work, "Contributions of Black People to the Kingdom of God," *Student World*, XVI (April, 1923), 43–45; Monroe N. Work, "The Negroes of Warsaw, Georgia," *Southern Workman*, XXXVII (January, 1908), 29–40; Monroe N. Work, "Self-Help Among the Negroes," *Survey*, August 7, 1909, pp. 616–18; Monroe N. Work, "Secret Societies as Factors in the Social and Economic Life of the Negro," *Proceedings of the Southern Sociological Congress* (1916).

25. Monroe N. Work, "The Spirit of Negro Poetry," *Southern Workman*, XXXVII (February, 1908), 73–77.

was well aware of the frustrations and handicaps of being black in a "white America." One area of limited opportunity especially distressing to Work was the status of black education, and he pointed out that although blacks constituted 11 percent of the United States population, they received only 2 percent of the total expenditures for education. He noted that in 1909 one northern educational institution had twice as large an income as the combined revenues of the nation's 123 black colleges and industrial schools and that in the southern states as a whole only $2.82 was spent on the education of each black child, as contrasted to $10.23 for each white child. He ironically described the situation by remarking that in some areas of the South convict labor rented out for more than black teachers were paid. In addition, Negro education was handicapped by shorter terms, inadequate facilities, and poorer teacher preparation. Work was especially concerned about the neglect of black education in the small unincorporated villages and towns that were virtually untouched by the philanthropic and public funds being applied to remedy the problems of urban and rural education.[26]

In respect to educational theory, Work held that there were two main functions of education. The first was to "assist in providing individuals with the ability to adapt themselves, collectively and singly, to existing conditions." This was not the same as the old Spencerian evolutionary formula, Work asserted, for the second function was to "provide individuals with the ability to assume an active, aggressive attitude towards environment—to change it, and make it adapt itself to their needs." He believed educators needed to put their responsibilities into perspective and to concentrate on the desired ends of education, rather than the physical means to obtain them. In black education in particular, he believed there was a twofold need. In keeping with Du Bois' theory of the Talented Tenth, he asserted that the first of these was to educate students for

26. Monroe N. Work, "Education of the Negro" (Typescript, 1910, in Box 3), Monroe N. Work, "The Status of Elementary Negro Education" (Typescript of address to the National Association of Teachers in Colored Schools in Petersburg, Va., July 23, 1930), Monroe N. Work, "An Educational No Man's Land" (Typescript of address to the N.A.T.C.S. in Orangeburg, S.C., August 1, 1919), both in Box 4, Work Papers.

the professions. The second need, encompassed in the ideals of Tuskegee Institute, was for a comprehensive scheme for the economic improvement of blacks. Black education must advance in both areas, Work believed, before black people could take their rightful place in American society.[27]

As a sociologist he examined the impact of current social and economic trends on black Americans. By far the most significant of these trends was the great population shift that was occurring. Work understood that black migration to the cities of both the North and South had profound implications. He predicted economic and political gains from this movement, but he was also aware that it created new problems and intensified some old ones. Both the statistical data he collected and his own experiences in Chicago and Savannah increased his concern about black urban problems. He noted that the city had a disruptive effect on family life because individual family members tended to engage in different kinds of occupations instead of working as a unit. Housing was a crucial problem, in his estimation, for blacks were frequently forced to live in unsanitary hovels or pay excessive rent that necessitated taking in boarders. Recreation was a problem, especially in the urban areas of the South, because blacks were excluded from most public recreational facilities and the church had been unable to maintain the central position in urban black social life that it held in rural areas. Poverty was a problem in both rural and urban locations, but it became more critical in the cities, for the trend toward individualism there often meant there was no one to look after the homeless and hungry. The rural Negro migrant, Work believed, was generally poorly equipped for urban life and poorly trained for urban employment. All of these disruptive factors, combined with the relaxation of the moral constraints applied in close-knit rural communities dominated by the church, helped to produce a high crime rate among urban blacks. But urban crime could have more serious consequences than the migrants were prepared for. In the rural South blacks seldom encountered the legal system unless they committed crimes against whites. In the city, however,

27. Work, "Problems of Education," 520–22, 525.

blacks were haled before a criminal justice system of which they had little knowledge and with which they were ill prepared to deal. Nevertheless, although the cost of the urban migration was high, Work believed that it was offset by the advantages of the growth of group leadership and the diversification of black occupations.[28]

The results of Work's long study of population changes and land tenure in the South were summarized in two speeches given before the Southern Sociological Society and published in *Social Forces*. In "Racial Factors and Economic Forces in Land Tenure in the South," he described a pattern of rural migration by both whites and blacks from counties with large black populations to predominantly white counties, resulting in a more even distribution of blacks in the region. Noting that the black counties were often in areas dominated by cotton production, he explained that the biracial emigration was probably the result of economic forces.[29]

In the patterns of landownership, however, the importance of racial factors was undeniable. Most of the black-owned farms were small, and they tended to be located in regions where the soil was less rich. Moreover, the amount of land owned by black farmers was steadily decreasing. This situation, Work argued, had largely resulted from discriminatory practices. Whites usually refused to sell property to blacks in predominantly white areas. In addition, racial factors were "a cause of uncertainty in Negro land ownership." Work explained, "There is always present the danger that if at any time trouble should arise between the Negro land owner and a white person, the Negro may be forced to leave the community and lose his holdings altogether or be compelled to dispose of them at a great sacrifice."[30]

Another problem arose relating to land titles that was "not so much a racial matter as an ignorant, a poor man's matter." Thousands of acres purchased by blacks had been lost because proper titles were not acquired. A major cause was the "bond-for-title"

28. Monroe N. Work, "Problems of Negro Urban Welfare," *Southern Workman*, LI (January, 1922), 10–16.

29. Monroe N. Work, "Racial Factors and Economic Forces in Land Tenure in the South, 1860–1930," *Social Forces*, XV (December, 1936), 205–215.

30. *Ibid.*

method wherein a contract between buyer and seller was signed requiring the purchaser to fulfill certain stipulations to acquire a deed. "Many an ignorant Negro," Work wrote, "because of its legal phraseology has considered his bond-for-title as an actual deed," although repossession of the title by whites was actually a relatively simple matter.[31]

An additional reason for the decline in black-owned farms was the inability of black banks and insurance companies to meet the mortgage needs of black farmers. In 1936 all black insurance companies combined held mortgages on less than six thousand acres, although in 1930 over three million acres of black-owned farmland were mortgaged. During the Depression, foreclosures increased, and the land usually passed into white hands.[32]

Work further elaborated the interaction of economic and racial factors in "Problems of the Adjustment of Race and Class in the South," which was published the same year as John Dollard's *Caste and Class in a Southern Town*. Work's major tenet was that the southern elite had used the concept of racial solidarity to promote its interest at the expense of all other groups. He sought to explain the origins of this manipulation of racial issues and its influence in keeping the region in poverty. He believed the doctrine of white supremacy had arisen from the special conditions of a frontier agricultural society and was no longer relevant in the emerging "industrial-commercial economy" of the South. Work traced the doctrine's roots to the minority position of whites among Indians and blacks during the frontier period of English southern settlement and to the need to justify slavery. As the planter class arose, it developed various forms of internal and external social control to promote its interest.

> External control, as attempted by the South, was mainly political in its aspects and consisted of the efforts of a conscious minority group to achieve and maintain advantages, mainly economic, through political manipulation and domination. . . . There was also the presence of a large group of subjected and exploited alien people, the Negroes. The problem of internal control, on the one hand, was

31. *Ibid.*
32. *Ibid.*

mainly through force to keep this alien group in its place; on the other hand, through manipulation, to control the interests and aspirations of the middle and poor white classes. Part of this manipulation consisted in emphasizing white solidarity. . . . This explains in part, at least, why the economic interests of poorer whites were subordinated; why their class consciousness remained undeveloped while at the same time their ideas of racial superiority attained a high degree of development.[33]

In the new industrializing South, such racial concepts were no longer useful, according to Work. Slavery no longer existed, whites were no longer a minority, and the agricultural elite was less important in the economy. Yet while southern industry became more national and international in scope, the large landowners continued to practice outmoded landlord-tenant relationships and wielded unwarranted political influence. Thus, the vestiges of the old order caused the South to lag behind the other sections of the nation economically and socially. To illustrate this point, Work noted the region's lower wages and its political isolation. During the 1936 presidential election, he remarked, "Southern democracy found itself somewhat in a class with the Negro. It was a minority in a national democratic party." If the South was to progress, Work asserted, outdated racial concepts must be replaced by a growing class consciousness. He left the ironic fact unstated that most interracial cooperation had occurred between upper-class blacks and whites within such organizations as the Commission on Interracial Cooperation and between blacks and whites of the lower classes in tenant farmers' and coal miners' unions. Few contacts existed between the black and white middle classes, whose emergence was a central feature in the New South.[34]

In his conclusions Work noted, "The Southern political order does not fit into the national political order, nor does the Southern moral order fit into the national moral order." White southerners, he argued, "are still attempting to maintain differences based on race; while at the same time the economic order with its industrial

33. Monroe N. Work, "Problems of Adjustment of Race and Class in the South," *Social Forces*, XVI (October, 1937), 108–17.
34. *Ibid.*

dominance is more or less impersonal and is operating to place on the same level all of the individuals in a particular class regardless of race." However, he foresaw a day when the new economy would "provide a situation in which there will be not only economic cooperation, but also cooperation between race and race, and between class and class, so that the interests of all people will be conserved."[35]

These conclusions highlighted Work's dream for the future. In his desire to eliminate outmoded white prejudice and to inspire black confidence, he wrote over seventy articles and delivered more than twice that many speeches. Considering his other duties and contributions, this activity is a remarkable testimony to his dedication. Very little that affected black existence was overlooked in his speeches and articles. Characteristically, he nevertheless considered his most important contribution to be his bibliography, in which he provided others with the tools to write and to speak.[36]

Work's articles tended to be brief and scantily documented, but not because they were inadequately researched. The succinct conclusions he published were usually the product of extensive research done within his department. For example, "Some Negro Members of Reconstruction Conventions and Legislatures and of Congress" was based upon more than three years of exhaustive correspondence with state archivists, county clerks, and the surviving public officials themselves, as well as their relatives. In "Aspects and Tendencies of the Race Problem," Work summed up in five pages the results of thirteen years of research on race relations. Although not published until the late 1930s, the *Social Forces* articles on race and class were based on more than ten years of research, part of which was done at the University of Chicago with the aid of historian William E. Dodd and sociologist Ellsworth Faris. After all this work, both articles together only numbered nineteen pages.[37]

Because of Work's conciseness, many of his articles are almost

35. *Ibid.*
36. Jessie P. Guzman, my interview, January 6, 1982.
37. Monroe N. Work, "Some Negro Members of Reconstruction Conventions and Legislatures and of Congress," *Journal of Negro History*, V (January,

devoid of interpretation and appear to jump from one statistic to another. It is partly a stylistic reflection of his belief in the power of facts to change opinions. Interpretations, he believed, can be challenged as propaganda, but facts are hard to refute. Thus, in his articles for professional journals, one has to look closely for a flicker of the man and his own thoughts on the subject. When he wrote for black audiences, however, and in his speeches, Work's own sentiments and theories are more easily recognized. From these, he emerges as a man intensely proud of his race but able to acknowledge its weaknesses and handicaps. He was determined to enlighten the dark corners of prejudice and discrimination so that blacks might be allowed to develop their full potential and make their unique contributions to civilization. The enormity of this task, in light of Work's belief that all social relations are interrelated, drove him in his relentless pursuit of facts with which to understand all facets of black existence. Such a pursuit is commendable in both a man and a scholar, but it tended to weaken his position in the field of sociology. The scope of his efforts, his timidity in drawing conclusions from his data, and the expenditure of the bulk of his time in providing research tools for others prevented his making a valuable contribution to sociological theory or producing a monograph—the accepted criteria for academic success. Thus, he has been practically ignored in more recent works on black sociologists and scholars.

Like many black scholars of his time, Work was forced by current conditions to become a "race man" and to devote his energies to defending and trying to uplift his fellow blacks. He utilized his talents to accomplish these goals but was not content to remain in academic isolation and merely write about race relations. After expressing a faith in black potential and a dream of a truly biracial America, Monroe Work actively engaged in projects to bring to fruition his hopes for his race and his country.

1920), 63–119; Monroe N. Work, "Aspects and Tendencies of the Race Problem," *Publications of the American Sociological Society*, XIX (1925), 191–96.

VI / Little Value Was Placed on the Life of an Individual Negro

While Monroe Work was at Savannah, he founded an organization that challenged the black elite "to come out of their closets of seclusion." Although he forsook overt protest to go to Tuskegee, he was not the type of man to retreat to such a closet. The conditions of the time did not allow the luxury of academic isolation to any concerned black. Knowledge was not sought for its own sake but as a tool for change. For a sociologist and educator, this meant aggressively seeking to distribute the truth to those who most needed it. Often these people were not in Tuskegee's classrooms and did not read professional journals. Thus, special channels of communication had to be created to reach them.

The Tuskegee environment encouraged such endeavors; Washington often stressed the goal of "making education common," that is, relating to the needs of the masses. His philosophy was the root of Tuskegee's many and varied extension activities in which Work quickly became involved. He served as secretary of the extension committee that sought to expand Tuskegee's impact beyond the classroom.

The seriousness of black health problems had long troubled Work, so he naturally sought to increase the efforts in that area. He clearly realized the devastating toll of illness and early death, especially among poor blacks. In 1913 the life expectancy of blacks in the United States was only thirty-five years. Almost every major illness claimed proportionately more black victims than white. Unlike most white scholars, Work did not believe these statistics reflected black genetic inferiority. He realized that poverty and ignorance were the major causes. Blacks were forced by economic conditions and discrimination to live in unhealthy environments and to eat nutritionally deficient diets, and their lack of resources limited their access to health care and knowledge. Work had faith that much could be done to alleviate these appalling conditions.

As president of the Savannah Men's Sunday Club, he had proposed a health campaign as one of the organization's first programs in 1905. The club persuaded black ministers to allow teams of physicians, dentists, and laymen to lecture during a part of the morning or evening worship services, and the "result was that in practically all of the churches large or small throughout the city the gospel of good health was presented to the people in a language so simple that the most ignorant could comprehend what was being said."[1]

It was probably not coincidental that the December after Work arrived in Tuskegee the campus newspaper announced a health week and encouraged black churches to give special attention to the "gospel of good health and right living." Work realized, however, that one of the most effective of Tuskegee's extension activities was the annual Negro Conference, established by Washington in 1892. Each year black farmers, teachers, and workers gathered on campus for instruction in ways to improve farming practices, educational opportunities, and social conditions. Beginning in 1909, Work was able to get a few sessions of the conference devoted to health. Characteristically, he hoped to construct a larger program from these humble beginnings.[2]

Using various tactics, he gradually convinced Washington of the possible effectiveness of an aggressive campaign to improve health conditions. In 1910 he informed the principal of his visits to the managers of the American Tobacco Company and the Durham Hosiery Mill, both in Durham, North Carolina, which had resulted in securing their cooperation with a local black hospital in sponsoring "a visiting nurse to work among the colored people . . . that

1. Monroe N. Work, "A Health Week in Savannah, Georgia, in 1902" (Typescript, October 14, 1930, in Box 2, Monroe Nathan Work Papers, Tuskegee Institute Archives).

2. Tuskegee *Student*, December 5, 1908; Monroe N. Work, "An Autobiographical Sketch" (MS, February 7, 1940, in Box 1, Work Papers).

their home life may be improved." The following year he suggested that Washington contact various local officials in Montgomery who had expressed an interest in improving sanitary conditions among blacks. At about the same time, he also proposed that more attention be given the subject at the annual conference. Six months later he couched his appeal in terms likely to stir Washington's interest. "I believe that the white papers of the South will lend their support to whatever effort we may make in this direction," he wrote. "I further believe that this would be a very effective method of increasing the interest of the white people of the South in Tuskegee Institute."[3]

Although Washington was undoubtedly concerned about black health problems, the issue for him was evidently not the burning obsession that it was for Work. The topic received some expanded attention at the annual conferences, but it was not until 1914 that the entire "Welfares Day" was devoted to the subject. At that session speeches were given by Dr. Oscar Dowling, president of the Louisiana State Board of Health; Dr. W. H. Sanders, president of the Alabama State Board of Health; Dr. A. M. Brown, president of the National Association of Negro Surgeons and Physicians; and Dr. E. T. Belsaw, president of the Alabama Negro Medical Association. The National Child Welfare Committee of New York maintained an exhibit at the conference illustrating ways to conserve the health of children, and the Louisiana State Board of Health sent its two Health Cars to show in graphic form how to improve sanitary conditions and combat disease.[4]

The charts prepared by Work's Department of Records and Research provoked the greatest amount of discussion. They showed that at any given time 456,000 blacks in the South were seriously ill. This meant an average loss of eighteen days of work a year for each black inhabitant. In monetary terms, sickness annually cost the South $75 million. According to the department's research,

3. Monroe Work to Booker T. Washington, December 19, 1910, in Box 604; January 7, 9, 24, July 31, 1911, all in Box 614, all in Booker T. Washington Papers, Library of Congress.
4. Work, "Autobiographical Sketch"; Monroe N. Work, *The South and the Conservation of Negro Health* (Tuskegee, 1915), 2.

half of the illnesses were preventable. If conditions were improved, the economic waste could be decreased and the black life expectancy of thirty-five years could be increased to fifty within fifty years.[5]

Monroe Work had endeavored to make the most of this opportunity, and his efforts were rewarded. At the end of the conference, it was resolved to establish a southeastern Negro health organization and to hold further conferences. Work published his charts in a pamphlet entitled *The South and the Conservation of Negro Health*, which was distributed to teachers and others to promote health improvement. He continued to inform Washington of individuals and groups who would be interested in a national movement. Finally, in the fall of 1914 the principal issued a call for the first National Negro Health Week. Its language reflected the influence of Work's concerns: "Without health and until we reduce the high death rate, it will be impossible for us to have permanent success in business, in property getting, in acquiring education, or to show other evidences of progress. Without health and long life, all else fails. We must reduce our high death rate, dethrone disease, enthrone health and long life. We may differ on other subjects, but there is no room for difference here. Let us make a strong, long, united pull together."[6]

Monroe Work was placed in charge of promoting the week, and he wrote the first *Health Week Bulletin*, outlining how it was to be observed. He realized that the first National Negro Health Week would have to be a success, in order for the program to continue and expand. Taking the position that health conservation was a public matter, Work wrote municipal, state, and national public health agencies, asking that they cooperate in the effort for health improvement. He persuaded the Alabama state medical officer, who was also president of the Southern Association of State Health

5. Monroe N. Work, "Tuskegee Institute: More Than an Educational Institution," *Journal of Educational Sociology*, VII (November, 1933), 202; Work, "Autobiographical Sketch."

6. Tuskegee *Student*, January 24, 1914; Monroe N. Work to Booker T. Washington, September 16, November 27, 1914, both in Box 653, Washington Papers; Monroe N. Work, "Booker T. Washington, Pioneer," *Journal of Social Forces*, III (January, 1925), 310–15.

Officers, to write all of his fellow health officers, pointing out the importance of the venture and asking their cooperation. The first National Negro Health Week was held in the spring of 1915 and was so successful that the National Negro Business League decided to sponsor its continuation.[7]

Booker T. Washington's death the following fall might have jeopardized the fragile new venture. However, the new principal, R. R. Moton, shared Work's interest in the issue. He had helped establish a similar movement on a local level as early as 1909, while he was at Hampton Institute. Thus, he quickly gave his support to National Negro Health Week, for which Work and the Department of Records and Research had already assumed primary responsibility.[8]

Under Work's leadership Negro Health Week grew into a national campaign. His department distributed literature to groups wishing to sponsor local health weeks. This printed matter mostly comprised handouts on good health practices, but there were also posters, suggestions for a health week sermon, and an outline of activities for the week. Typical activities included: School Health Day, on which health care professionals would visit the local schools to educate and examine the children; Sanitation Day, which involved citizens in a systematic attack on areas with stagnant water that bred mosquitoes; and General Clean Up Day, on which special efforts were made to clean homes, schools, and public buildings and their surroundings. By the 1920s hundreds of communities were participating, and at Work's suggestion, National Negro Health Week was formally designated to coincide with Booker T. Washington's birthday.[9]

As Negro Health Week grew into a national movement, the expense of promoting it also increased. In 1922 Work had a conference with Dr. C. C. Pierce, acting surgeon general of the United

7. Work, "Autobiographical Sketch"; Tuskegee *Student*, October 13, 1917.

8. Copy of article sent to Roscoe C. Brown, [1934], in Box LC63, Robert Russa Moton Papers, Tuskegee Institute Archives.

9. Fifteenth Annual Negro Health Week (Brochure, in "Health Week, 1929," Department of Records and Research Files, Tuskegee Institute Archives); Minutes of the Executive Council (in Tuskegee Institute Archives), January 20, 1920; Tuskegee *Student*, February 12, 1921.

States. As a result of this meeting, the United States Public Health Service took over the expense of publishing literature for the observation of the week, and Dr. Roscoe C. Brown was assigned to participate in the activities. After 1922 the surgeon general held annual meetings in his own office to formulate plans for health week observance; Work provided the agenda for the meetings.[10]

Work's efforts did not stop with getting the federal government involved in the movement. He actively sought the cooperation of health-related groups and state governments, as well. Although he was not very successful with the American Red Cross, he did obtain the cooperation of the National Clean-Up and Paint-Up Bureau, which awarded a silver cup to the rural community, the city with fewer than 100,000 residents, and the city whose population exceeded 100,000 for the best showing in health week activities. In 1921 the governor of Georgia issued an official proclamation in support of the week.[11]

Not content with a successful health week each year, Work dreamed of a year-round health program for Negroes. He worked continuously to persuade state health departments to undertake this task. Finally, in 1930 the United States Public Health Service, in cooperation with the Julius Rosenwald Fund, took over National Negro Health Week and, changing its name to National Negro Health Movement, made the program year-round.[12]

Soon afterwards the paternity of Negro Health Week was obscured. Moton claimed that Washington had gotten the idea from his Virginia program. Other people and organizations had launched public health campaigns earlier, including the all-black National Medical Association and Meharry Medical College in Nashville, Tennessee. Yet Monroe Work is clearly the primary father of this

10. Work, "Autobiographical Sketch"; Work to Robert R. Moton, May 28, 1926, in Box LC43, Moton Papers.

11. Tuskegee *Student*, March 31, 1917, March 26, 1921; Philip Klein to Work, February 8, 1921, W. Frank Persons to Work, February 23, 1921, both in Box 18, Thomas M. Campbell Papers, Tuskegee Institute Archives.

12. Work to Moton, November 11, 1919, in Box LC22, Moton Papers; Work, "Autobiographical Sketch"; "The What and Why of National Negro Health Week," in *National Negro Health Week: Twentieth Anniversary* (Washington, D.C., 1934), 6.

specific movement, which helped to coordinate and expand the earlier endeavors. Not only was he instrumental in its conception, but he also nurtured it to maturity. As was often the case, he seemed willing to step into the shadows as long as his goals were met.

To further the cause, Work also gave numerous speeches at various conferences outlining the need for health improvement among blacks. To southern whites he stressed the economic loss caused by black illness and death, pointing out that during slavery each slave represented a large investment to his master, who therefore valued his life. "After Emancipation, however, and the doing away of personal ownership," he declared, "little value was placed on the life of an individual Negro, for it was reasoned that if one died another could be had to take his place." Only after the new emphasis on conserving natural resources, Work said, had communities realized the financial loss created by the death of their members.[13]

In 1924, ten years after the establishment of Negro Health Week, Work was able to make an encouraging report on the state of black health. The death rate per thousand had dropped from 24.2 to 16—a 33.8 percent decrease for blacks, as compared to a 22.7 percent decrease for whites during the same period. Although the death rate for whites was still lower than that for blacks, Negroes were clearly making progress. This was further indicated, Work pointed out, in the fact that during the same ten years the average black life expectancy had increased some five years. In summarizing the situation, Work quoted a statistician of the Metropolitan Life Insurance Company:

> The lengthening of expected life span is one of the aims of public health work and who shall say that such an effort has not succeeded to an extent wholly unexpected by the most enthusiastic of the workers in this field ten years ago. . . . The addition of a single year to the span of life is a stupendous achievement implying, as it does, the addition of millions of years of productive effort in the aggregate for the wage working population. When the life span of a people lengthens as much as five years in a single decade it is indicative of

13. Monroe N. Work, "The South and Negro Health" (Typescript of an address to the Southern Sociological Congress in Houston, Tex., 1915, in Box 4, Work Papers).

far-reaching changes in the conditions of life and labor. There is no longer any room for gloomy pessimism respecting the Negro's chance for survival. The members of this race have benefitted decidedly and are improving their longevity prospect constantly from wider economic opportunity and from public health measures.

Five years later Work was able to report that the black life span had increased another two years.[14]

Because of his efforts in the field of health, Work was appointed as the only black consultant in statistical studies by the National Tuberculosis Association. But by far the greatest tribute to Work's dream was that his optimistic goal of a fifty-year black life expectancy by 1964 had been surpassed before his death in 1945. By 1941 the life expectancy of black males was more than fifty-two years.[15]

Monroe Work perceived the vital importance of the Negro health movement, but he also recognized another threat to the lives of blacks—lynching. At the beginning of the twentieth century, lynchings had come to average more than one a week. Before the Civil War, lynching had been primarily a response to frontier conditions and the lack of access to the legal justice system; it generally did not involve blacks. After the war, however, the racial bias in lynching became more and more apparent. From 1882 to 1930, 4,761 persons were lynched, 71 percent of them black. Although only six states did not have a lynching during this period, the problem was more acute in the South where 3,810 victims—3,136 blacks and 674 whites—met their death at the hands of lynch mobs.[16]

The cause of this racially and sectionally biased outburst of

14. Monroe N. Work, "Morbidity and Mortality of the Negro Race from a Statistical Standpoint" (Typescript of an address to the John Andrews Clinical Society in Tuskegee, Ala., April 3, 1924), Monroe N. Work, "The Economic Waste of Sickness" (Typescript of an address to the Health Conference in Gulfpride, Miss., June 5, 1929), both in Box 3, Work Papers.

15. Washington *Tribune*, August 27, 1921 (Clipping in Box 2, Work Papers); U.S. Department of Health, Education, and Welfare, *Vital Statistics of the United States, 1961* (Washington, D.C., 1964), 2–11.

16. Monroe N. Work (ed.), *Negro Year Book, 1931–32* (Tuskegee, 1932), 293; See Arthur F. Raper, *The Tragedy of Lynching* (New York, 1933); James E. Cutler, *Lynch-Law* (New York, 1905); Walter White, *Rope and Faggot: A Biography of Judge Lynch* (New York, 1929); Southern Commission for the study of Lynching, *Lynchings and What They Mean* (n.p., n.d.); James H. Chadbourne, *Lynching and the Law* (Chapel Hill, 1933).

lynching has long been debated. Some have noted the South's long-standing penchant for violence. Others have seen blacks as scapegoats, and lynching as an outlet for the economic and political frustrations of southern whites. Since lynch mobs were usually composed of lower-class whites, economic competition for too few jobs has also been cited as a cause. All these factors probably contributed to the situation, but lynching seems to have been primarily a form of racial control, a way to keep blacks "in their place." So long as slavery served that purpose, lynching was relatively rare. As Work noted, the ownership of blacks gave their lives economic value; therefore, the whip and other incentives brought slaves under control, and the threat of enslavement was usually effective with free blacks. Slavery also elevated even the poorest whites above the bottom rung of society.

Lynching, along with legal segregation, helped to forge a new caste system after the demise of slavery. The economic benefits of such a caste system were, of course, enormous—at least to the southern white elite. To the poorer whites, the gains were largely psychological. As Monroe Work asserted in his article on race and class, the doctrine of white supremacy had developed in part to justify slavery. Ideology is usually rooted in perceived economic needs, but in time, ideas can acquire a life of their own and become so fervently believed that people will make great financial sacrifices to uphold them. Such was the case with the concept of black inferiority. Many whites sincerely believed and deeply feared that a serious genetic degeneration would flow from miscegenation. Since white men had made black women victims of their lust and aggression for centuries, white women were seen as the key to racial purity. Thus, a great cult arose regarding the southern woman. She was to be cherished and not defiled except for the procreation of the master race.

At the same time, a misunderstanding of black sexual mores and the need for respite from their own puritanical sexual standards led whites to project onto blacks most of their taboo fantasies. Blacks were viewed as the purely sensual creatures that whites longed to be. Because white men desired black women, they presumed that all black men wanted the forbidden fruit of white women. The black male was depicted as a raging bull, restrained from raping white women only by fear.

These ideas provided strong support for the practice of lynching. Many whites asserted that mob justice was a necessary deterrent to black rape and believed lynchings to be a "sort of natural outburst, in some ways a strong man's gesture, splashed liberally with knight errantry and designed to protect the blushing flower of Southern womanhood."[17] Even when the real "offense" might be a black's bringing suit against whites or merely his boasting, charges of rape were often fabricated to inspire a lust for revenge and to quiet investigation.

Racially motivated lynchings tended to be especially grisly. Although victims were most commonly hanged, revenge-seeking mobs also resorted to shooting, beating, burning at the stake, and drowning. Often the accused was viciously tortured before being killed. Some suffered sexual mutilation; the loss of fingers, toes, and ears; or the heat of blow torches on bare chest. Anything was justified for the sake of white supremacy.

Lynching was undoubtedly the most barbarous consequence of erroneous racial stereotypes and was thus of special interest to Monroe Work. He first became aware of the extent of the problem about 1900, while he was still a student at Chicago and read a detailed account of lynchings in the Chicago *Tribune*. He immediately started collecting records of lynchings, but only after he came to Tuskegee did he have the facilities to compile the data in a systematic manner. At the time, the *Tribune* was the only agency regularly collecting and publishing lynching statistics; a few articles and James E. Cutler's *Lynch-Law* (1905) were the only other major sources of publicity about this evil. Work decided none of this information was receiving enough attention; the annual reports of the *Tribune* were being ignored, he believed, because of the reluctance of competing papers to credit their source.[18] He felt sure

17. John R. Clowes, "The People's Crime," Louisville *Courier-Journal* Sunday Magazine, March 10, 1940, p. 1, as cited in Henry Eugene Barber, "The Association of Southern Women for the Prevention of Lynching, 1930–1942" (M.A. thesis, University of Georgia, 1967), 7.

18. Monroe N. Work, "Thirty Years of the Tuskegee Lynching Records" (Typescript, 1938, in Box 5, Work Papers), 4; Work to Washington, December 30, 1910, in Box 614, Washington Papers.

that other newspapers would publish material on lynching only if it came to them from an independent source.

Lynching had long been a concern of Booker T. Washington, who had sometimes issued public letters on the subject. As early as 1910, Work was regularly sending lynching data to the principal, and he prepared a report on the lynchings of 1912 for distribution. This endeavor met with some opposition at Tuskegee Institute, for both Robert E. Park and Emmett J. Scott believed that the Department of Records and Research did not have the facilities to compete with the *Tribune*. Not easily discouraged, Work took the report directly to Washington, who readily agreed to send it to the Chicago *Herald*, in the hope that the *Herald* would gladly accept it in order to compete with the *Tribune*. Thus, Work took the first step toward his real purpose of making lynching statistics more widely read, and once again he used a small opportunity as a springboard to greater things.[19]

Work began compiling semiannual lynching reports, and by 1914, these were being sent to some three hundred daily newspapers, the Associated Press, and all the leading black papers. In 1915 the *World Almanac* began publishing Work's record of lynchings. His goal was beginning to be fulfilled, but he knew that the sentiment in favor of lynchings was strongest in southern rural districts, which were still not being reached with the facts. Consequently, beginning in 1922, the lynching report was sent to some two thousand country newspapers, mainly in the South. Many of the editors first greeted the reports with some degree of hostility, but they were soon appeased with the idea of receiving the same sort of service as metropolitan newspapers.[20]

Actually, resentment was fairly easily allayed because of Work's approach to the compilation and distribution of his lynching statistics. Firmly believing that "no sort of propaganda is, in the end, so effective as the facts themselves," he relied on the data to deliver his message. The reports were sent with little editorial comment, and all followed the same format. First, he gave the total number of

19. Monroe N. Work, interview by Lewis A. Jones, May 15, 1932 (Transcript in Box 1, Jessie P. Guzman Papers, Tuskegee Institute Archives), hereinafter cited as Jones interview.

20. Work, "Autobiographical Sketch."

lynchings for the year or half year and a comparison of those figures with the lynchings of the two previous years. Next, he categorized the incidents by the race of the victims and the nature of their reported offenses. Since one of his primary purposes was to illustrate that the majority of lynchings were not for the "one great cause," he would then give the percentage of lynchings for the reason of rape. The reports closed with a breakdown of lynchings by state and after 1913 included a report on lynchings that had been prevented, if any. Later, he added statistics on the indictments, convictions, and sentences of lynchers to indicate the appalling laxity of the legal system in combating this evil. Sometimes the report detailed particularly gruesome lynchings; occasionally it included known instances of the murder of innocent people. Generally, the reports were signed by the principal.[21]

In compiling the figures released in these reports, Work relied on the newspapers and other resources processed by the Department of Records and Research. Any mention of lynching in any source would be noted and, if questionable, checked by correspondence. Since Tuskegee was widely considered the center of all things relating to the Negro, reports of lynchings not mentioned in the newspapers would come from interested correspondents. Once verified, they were included in the statistics for the year. As with all the material in his files, the lynching information was systematically categorized every year. The headings comprised reported cases, lynchings prevented, legal punishment of lynchers, discussions of lynchings, NAACP report on lynching, rapes by whites, and sidelights.[22]

Thanks to Work's painstaking research methods and factual presentations, the Tuskegee Lynching Report gained wide acceptance. In time all other leading compilers of lynching statistics referred their records to the Department of Records and Research for collabo-

21. Monroe N. Work, "The Importance of Exact Race Knowledge" (Typescript of an address to the All Races Conference in Chicago, Ill., February 13, 1924, in Box 4, Work Papers); Work, "Thirty Years," 4–8; Work to Moton, July 2, 1921, in Box LC26, Moton Papers.
22. Monroe N. Work, "Using a Collection of Materials on the Negro" (Typescript of an address given at Fisk University, November 11, 1930, in Box 4, Work Papers); Work, "Thirty Years," 16.

ration before they were published. The *American Year Book* and the *International Year Book* joined the *World Almanac* in publishing Work's data. The files were also used by ministers for sermons and by professors for articles and speeches. But the most widespread use of his statistics was by the press. During 1932, for example, more than two hundred editorial comments on the Tuskegee Lynching Report appeared in newspapers and magazines.[23]

Most important, since lynching was primarily a problem in the South, Work's statistics were widely accepted as accurate by the southern press. For example, the Birmingham *Age-Herald* called him a "painstaking statistician" and declared his reports were "accepted everywhere as trustworthy." In an editorial denouncing Georgia's leading position in lynching for the year, the Atlanta *Constitution* said the report "is accepted as being authentic as the accuracy of its statistics in this respect has never been assailed." Work believed that southern acceptance made his lynching report the most valuable of the three then being issued. The Chicago *Tribune* continued its coverage and the NAACP began issuing similar reports about 1918. Work did not claim to be the first to publish the data, but he did note that the other agencies "were all outside the South" and their reports were perceived as "in general a criticism of the South." Thus, "the South assumed a more or less defensive attitude towards the evil and in many instances sought to justify it." A 1928 editorial in the Montgomery *Advertiser* confirmed Work's belief by declaring that "the National Association [for the Advancement of Colored People] is a propaganda society" and concluding, "We have always found the Tuskegee records to be reliable."[24]

Work was especially pleased that even small-town southern

23. Moton to James R. Angell, November 17, 1920, in Box LC22, Moton Papers; H. R. Arnold to Secretary of Tuskegee Institute, March 7, 1916, Work to Josiah Morse, February 10, 1916, *Survey*, May 20, 1916 (Clipping), all in Box 2, Work to George E. Haynes, January 16, 1929, in Box 18, all in Tuskegee Institute Lynching Records, Tuskegee Institute Archives; "Report to the General Board of Education on the Work of the Department of Records and Research of Tuskegee Institute for the Years 1932–1933" (Typescript, n.d., in Box 1, Work Papers).

24. Moton to Angell, November 17, 1920, in Box LC22, Moton Papers; Work, "Tuskegee Institute," 205; quoted in Tuskegee *Messenger*, February 11, 1928.

newspapers used his statistics and editorialized against lynching. For example, the Newton (Mississippi) *Record* condemned mob justice by asserting, "We cannot be true to our professions of citizenship if we put a finger on one law and say we favor it and will observe it, and put a finger on another law and say that we oppose it and will ignore it. . . . We have got to stand for the law in its entirety, not just for part of it. If we don't, the whole law will eventually go down before the onslaughts of its enemies, and the mob will be supreme."[25]

Sometimes Work's data was used in more controversial ways. In 1919, when Governor Hugh Dorsey of Georgia requested lynching statistics from the director of the state archives, the director turned to Work for the information. Dorsey used those statistics to produce a pamphlet entitled *As to the Negro in Georgia* in April, 1921. The booklet condemned various forms of mistreatment of the state's black population, creating a furor that led to the formation of a short-lived Dixie Defense League. Also, lawyers in the famous Scottsboro case worked several nights at Tuskegee using Work's files to aid their defense of the black boys charged with rape.[26]

Occasionally, Tuskegee's statistics were questioned or challenged. One of the reasons for such challenges was the very effectiveness of Work's reports. State and local officials, loath to see their localities receive negative publicity, would question the classification of a particular incident in their domain as a lynching. Some would politely request details of the case, while others would pressure Work to change the records. Complaints of this kind came from the governors of Virginia, South Carolina, Georgia, Alabama, Mississippi, and Texas. The superintendent of public instruction of North Carolina even offered to pay the expenses of a Tuskegee representative to conduct an investigation of an alleged lynching in Gaston County, North Carolina. On a few occasions, Work agreed with the officials after learning more about the incident and changed the record. But, in most cases, when the facts were presented, the

25. Quoted in Work, "Thirty Years," 26–27.
26. Jessie P. Guzman, "Monroe Nathan Work and His Contributions," *Journal of Negro History*, XXXIV (October, 1949), 450–51; Work, "Thirty Years," 36; Hugh Dorsey to Keeper of the Records, June 7, 1921, in Box LC26, Moton Papers.

officials would acquiesce; and even when pressure was applied, Work politely refused to change any records he knew to be true. The reluctance of these officials to have a lynching charged against their town or state nevertheless indicated the growing antilynching sentiment.[27]

Not all of the correspondents, however, believed lynchings were a blot on their localities. In 1924 R. R. Moton received an interesting letter signed "Savannah." The barely literate writer was dismayed at the small number of lynchings charged against Georgia during the first half of that year and noted: "Your report upon Lynchings is being well bosted over the country especially by that dirty sheet the Was Post. That low estimate 5 based upon the fact that 4 negro brutes who committed the usual crime in this community escaped in the past 3 months. Otherwise the number lynched would have been doubled. we will endeavor to make up for difincie. No man in George wants to Lynch. We want the crime *stoped*. Have you ever made an appeal to a negro audiance to stop it."[28]

Another kind of complaint stemmed from the fact that there was no nationally accepted definition of what constituted a lynching. Work sometimes found his statistics simultaneously assailed by those who insisted he had included incidents not properly classified as lynchings and others who felt he had erred in excluding others. Deciding where to draw the line was difficult not only for a statistician but also for a legislator. The difficulties encountered in drawing up a strict legal definition of lynching to go into antilynching bills can readily be seen in the sorts of cases not covered by most of such definitions.

Sometimes, for example, a mob killed with the authority of the law. Sheriffs might swear private citizens in as a posse. If such a posse captured and killed the suspect and then mutilated his body, some would say that they were simply overzealous in carrying out their duty, that this was a "legal lynching." Since a posse of twenty or thirty armed men who apprehended a lone suspect could reason-

27. Work, "Autobiographical Sketch"; Work, "Thirty Years," 39–64; N. C. Newbold to Work, September 23, 1941, in Box 2, Work Papers.

28. "Savannah" to Moton, July 7, 1924, in Box 11, Tuskegee Lynching Records.

ably be expected to be able to return him to prison alive, Work held this kind of incident to be a lynching and not the result of due process of law.

If a maimed body was found, perhaps in the woods or a river, it was difficult to say whether a single murderer or a lynch mob was responsible. Work took the position that the nature of death determined whether it was a lynching or not. Since it was improbable that one man could or would mutilate a body, tie it up, weight it, and throw it in a river, such incidents were listed as lynchings in his reports.

A mob that killed under the pretext of service to race or tradition when there was no misdemeanor or felony charged against the victim posed even more serious difficulties to the classifier. The question was whether mob action in the form of race riots should be included as lynchings. In this instance Work based his decision on the distinction between the indiscriminate killing of people and the killing of particular individuals for alleged offenses, whether criminal or not. The latter he designated as lynchings; the former he did not. Work also held that at least three people had to be involved before they could be considered to form a lynch mob.[29]

Because some of the bloodiest race riots against blacks occurred in the North, many southerners believed that the exclusion of riot victims from the statistics gave a distorted image of race relations in the nation. The NAACP also criticized Work's refusal to include race riot victims, and a sometimes bitter controversy erupted between Work and that civil rights organization. Realizing that the discrepancies between his lynching reports and the NAACP's gave the prolynching forces propaganda material, Work offered to cooperate with the association in coordinating them. Almost immediately, however, Work became disillusioned with these efforts and charged that the NAACP was using the statistics he supplied for its own advancement. Other attempts at cooperation also failed, for the NAACP believed Work was being too conservative in his definition of lynching, and he asserted that the NAACP was "not interested so much in accuracy as they were in propaganda."[30]

29. Work to Will W. Alexander, April 5, 1924, in Box LC55, Moton Papers.
30. James Weldon Johnson to Work, December 23, 1925, Work to Johnson, December 29, 1925, both in Box 13, Johnson to Work, December 12, 1928, Work

Work was especially concerned that including race riot victims in lynching statistics would cloud the issue and make passage of federal antilynching legislation more difficult. He refused at first to publicize his criteria for designating a lynching because he believed "there is danger of such a discussion taking very much the form of the present theological discussion dividing people into modernists and fundamentalists wheras [sic] the important thing is to have them united in an effort to supress all forms of mob violence."[31]

The controversy raged for more than ten years before any agreement was reached. Finally, on December 11, 1940, Frederick D. Patterson, president of Tuskegee Institute, called a meeting of antilynching leaders to determine the criteria to be used by both Tuskegee and the NAACP in compiling their lynching reports. A group of prominent editors, educators, and interracial leaders— along with Walter White, the secretary of the NAACP, and Monroe Work—agreed on a definition that stated: "There must be legal evidence that a person has been killed, and that he met his death illegally at the hands of a group acting under the pretext of service to justice, race, or tradition."[32]

Yet, not all of the discrepancies in the three major reports arose from disagreement over the definition of lynching. Local officials sometimes suppressed information about mob violence. The agencies were then forced to receive their information through unofficial channels not equally accessible to all of them. Also, obscure incidents were sometimes overlooked. Although Work and the NAACP occasionally cooperated successfully to discern the truth about a particular event, the relationship between the compiler of the *Tribune* records and Tuskegee was much more productive.[33]

---

to Johnson, December 22, 1928, both in Box 17, Walter White to Work, July 22, 1929, Work to White, July 25, 1929, both in Box 18, W. E. B. Du Bois to Work, January 10, 1931, Work to Du Bois, January 19, 1931, both in Box 22, all in Tuskegee Lynching Records; Work to Du Bois, January 4, 11, 1928, both in Box LC48, Moton Papers; Jones interview.

31. Work to Alexander, April 11, 1924, as cited in Work, "Thirty Years," 81.

32. Jessie Daniel Ames, *The Changing Character of Lynching* (Atlanta, 1942), 29.

33. Work to John R. Shilladay, July 12, 1919, R. G. Randolph to Work, July 31, 1919, both in Box 4, White to Work, April 29, 1924, Work to White, May 3, 1924, both in Box 13, all in Tuskegee Lynching Records; Work, "Thirty Years," 10–15, 17–25.

One area in which Work and the NAACP were able to work together was in the push for federal antilynching legislation. The civil rights group, although it investigated individual incidents and sponsored an antilynching conference in 1919, generally concentrated its efforts in the legislative sphere. Work did not subscribe to the NAACP doctrine that "nothing will stop [lynching] but Federal law," but he did prepare a statement for distribution to congressmen when the Dyer antilynching bill was debated in 1924. The handout was full of sober statistics, Work's favorite tool of suasion. "From the best and most accurate sources of information," he wrote, for example, "it is found that in the thirty-eight years, 1885–1923, there were 855 persons, 60 white and 795 Negroes put to death by mobs, under the charge of rape. This is one-fifth or 20.4 percent of the total number of persons, 4,183, who were lynched during that period. On the other hand, 3,328 or four-fifths of those lynched were for causes other than rape. This refutes the charge that the majority of lynchings were for the crime of rape."[34]

Still, the sporadic dissension between two of the leading antilynching forces tended to mar the entire endeavor. Moreover, it is somewhat surprising in view of the earlier close ties between Du Bois and Work. The blame for the failure to cooperate probably belongs to both men. Work may have been eager to prove the legitimacy of his conversion to Tuskegee. On the other hand, Du Bois seemed as reluctant to grant legitimacy to Tuskegee's programs as Washington had been to recognize the Niagara Movement. Du Bois once wrote Will Alexander about the interracial group that Alexander headed, which had close ties to Tuskegee. He noted, "Our greatest objection to the Interracial Commission is the kind of Negro you pick to go on it." He was also reluctant to share credit for the antilynching movement. In his 1925 article "Who Checked Lynching?" he did not mention Tuskegee and gave scant attention to the southern-based antilynching efforts before proclaiming, "But the NAACP with the Dyer bill put the fear of God into the Southern mob."[35]

34. W. E. B. Du Bois, "Who Checked Lynching?" *Crisis*, XXXIX (February, 1925), 154; Work, "Importance of Exact Race Knowledge." See Robert L. Zangrando, *The NAACP Crusade Against Lynching, 1909–1950* (Philadelphia, 1980).

35. Wilma Dykeman and James Stokely, *Seeds of Southern Change: The Life*

Although the NAACP spent large sums of money on the anti-lynching crusade and had a profound impact, it is doubtful that the organization's continuous unsuccessful preoccupation with federal legislation was as effective as the work of some southerners whose goals were primarily educational and many of whom had closer relationships with Monroe Work. A number of individuals, including McClellan Van de Veer of the Birmingham *Age-Herald*, Ralph McGill of the Atlanta *Constitution*, and George Fort Milton of the Chattanooga *News*, became Work's allies. In addition, several groups dedicated to the eradication of lynch-law found their inspiration in Work's data and relied upon his research skills to provide them with the tools to wage their battles.[36]

One of the most important of these was Will Alexander's Commission on Interracial Cooperation, headquartered in Atlanta. It had been organized by southern whites after a bloody rise in racial tensions following World War I, and its major purpose was the general improvement of race relations by bringing together black and white leaders and conducting educational campaigns. Tuskegee people naturally became involved, and in 1925 Monroe Work addressed the group on the subject of lynching. The CIC became especially alarmed when the number of lynchings rose dramatically in 1930. The commission established the Southern Commission for the Study of Lynchings to investigate all the lynchings of that year, as well as other aspects of mob violence, and Work was among the distinguished southern leaders appointed to the group. The results of their endeavors included a pamphlet entitled *Lynchings and What They Mean*, Arthur Raper's *The Tragedy of Lynching*, and James H. Chadbourne's *Lynching and the Law*.[37]

One of the CIC's greatest contributions, however, was the development of a separate, very effective antilynching group. The direc-

of Will Alexander (New York, 1962), 131; Du Bois, "Who Checked Lynching?" 154.

36. Ames, *Lynching*, 29; SCSL, *Lynchings and What They Mean*, 6.

37. See Jacquelyn Dowd Hall, *Revolt Against Chivalry* (New York, 1979); Edward Flud Burrows, "The Commission on Interracial Cooperation, 1919–1944: A Case Study in the Interracial Movement in the South" (Ph.D. dissertation, University of Wisconsin, 1955); Ann Wells Ellis, "The Commission on Interracial Cooperation, 1919–1944: Its Activities and Results" (Ph.D. dissertation, University of Georgia, 1975).

tor of women's work, Jessie Daniel Ames, believed that the best means of destroying the rape myth was for southern women to take a stand against lynching. To accomplish this end, she obtained funds from the commission to establish the Association of Southern Women for the Prevention of Lynching and called upon several dozen women to meet November 1, 1930, in Atlanta. At this meeting statistics supplied by Work were used to show that only 21 percent of the lynchings since 1886 had been for crimes against women. As Ames later wrote, "In a tense moment the women saw what had been traditionally known as Southern chivalry stripped to sadistic barbarism."[38]

Together, the Commission on Interracial Cooperation and the ASWPL launched educational drives against lynching. By the 1940s, the ASWPL alone had distributed over forty different pieces of literature and obtained antilynching endorsements from more than a hundred women's groups and twelve hundred southern peace officers. The two groups united to bring pressure on law enforcement officials whenever a lynching situation arose, and at Work's suggestion, the commission awarded medals to sheriffs who had shown courage or ingenuity in defending prisoners.[39]

Monroe Work was definitely a powerful, if somewhat silent, force in the campaign to eradicate lynching, and a number of other organizations concerned with race relations and lynching sought his advice and support. Among these were the Commission on Race Relations of the Federal Council of Churches, which published a pamphlet by Work called *The Law Versus the Mob*; the Boards of Home Missions of the Congregational and Christian churches; the University Commission on Southern Race Questions; the Chicago Commission on Race Relations; and the Southern Sociological Congress. Behind the scenes, in his usual quiet manner, he supplied the data that others used to demonstrate the destructive and repressive power of disrespect for the law.

Work also utilized the platforms provided by his articles and speeches to attack myths about lynching. Even many white liberals believed that a high black crime rate was at the root of lynching and

38. Ames, *Lynching*, 64.
39. *Ibid.*, 66–67; Work, "Thirty Years," 31.

that educated blacks should concentrate on reducing black crime. Work was realistic enough to acknowledge that better race relations were dependent on black as well as white respect for the law. In fact, he had become concerned with the problem of Negro crime even before his active interest in lynching. Freely admitting that the black crime rate was higher than the white, he devoted much effort to seeking solutions to this perplexing problem. Nevertheless, he refused to accept the widely held position that the only way to stop lynching was for the "better elements" among blacks to see that Negro crime was reduced and Negro criminals were not sheltered from the law. This, Work asserted, was to shift the "burden of policing from the police authorities and to place it upon respectable Negroes," a task that was not expected of the white elite.[40]

In any case, Work was convinced that lynching was not dependent on black disrespect for the law for a number of reasons. During his studies of Negro crime, for example, he had discovered that the black crime rate was higher in the North, although the majority of lynchings occurred in the South. Also, the black crime rate was lower than that of recent immigrant groups, but few immigrants were lynched. The charge that the high incidence of rape among Negroes was a chief cause of lynching was particularly absurd, for although the black rate was higher for all other crimes, it was actually lower than the white rate for rape. Work knew the myth that crime was endemic to the Negro race to be false because the crime rate in Haiti was one of the lowest in the world. Part of the problem in the United States, he believed, was that too often the black man looked upon the law "not as something made for his protection and designed to promote his welfare, but as something which is primarily to do him an injury."[41]

As in the case of black life expectancy, the statistics on lynching had significantly improved by the time of Work's death. By 1945 lynching had largely lost its terrible grip on American society. From

40. Monroe N. Work, "Crime Among the Negroes of Chicago," *American Journal of Sociology*, VI (September, 1900), 204–23; Monroe N. Work (ed.), *Negro Year Book, 1918–1919* (Tuskegee, 1919), 73.

41. Monroe N. Work, "Negro Criminality in the South," *Annals of the American Academy of Political and Social Sciences*, XLIX (September, 1913), 74–80; Monroe N. Work, "The Negro in the New World" (Typescript, n.d., in Box 3, Work Papers).

1882 to 1945, nearly five thousand people lost their lives to lynch mobs; during the following thirty-five years lynchings averaged well below one a year. The total number of lynchings since 1945 is less than half the number that occurred in the single year of 1912, when Work began his lynching reports.[42] Lynch-law might conceivably have died a natural death with the development of a more sophisticated society, but to expect such a solution would have been as illogical as expecting ignorance, or crime itself, to pass away of its own accord. Until a problem is recognized, it cannot be solved. Monroe Work helped bring this hideous practice into the light of national publicity and exploded the myths that supported its existence.

Another important result of Work's antilynching activities was to get him involved in the interracial movement of the South. He actively cooperated with the CIC in other aspects of its work and participated in other interracial groups that had been established before the Atlanta organization. The Southern Sociological Congress was founded in 1912 in Nashville, Tennessee, to bring together intellectuals to discuss the problems of the South. At the first meeting no blacks were on the program, but the group quickly decided that one of the region's major problems was race relations. The participation of blacks gradually increased, and in 1915 Monroe Work was one of six blacks presenting papers. That meeting started his lifetime affiliation with the group.[43]

Another organization whose interracial work preceded the CIC was the Young Men's Christian Association. Indeed, many of the founders of the CIC, including Willis D. Weatherford and Will Alexander, were active members of the YMCA. Weatherford, a white Texan, was an early and outspoken champion of racial justice. In 1916 he had presented Work's lynching statistics to the Southern Sociological Congress, and the following year he spon-

42. Daniel T. Williams, "The Lynching Records at Tuskegee Institute," in *Eight Negro Bibliographies* (New York, 1970), 8–11.

43. Work to Arthur Raper, May 14, 1921, in Box LC26, Moton Papers; Raper to Work, September 16, 1927, in Box 2, Alexander to Work, June 11, 1929, in Box 1, both in Work Papers; Work to Washington, May 24, 1915, in Box 664, Washington Papers; "The Southern Sociological Congress and the Race Problem" (Typescript, n.d., in Box 3, Work Papers).

sored a Law and Order Conference at a YMCA conference center he headed in Blue Ridge, North Carolina. As might be expected, Work became active in YMCA efforts, too.[44]

There were numerous other small-scale, local movements in which Work participated. He was involved in several statewide interracial organizations, serving as the recording secretary of groups in Alabama and Tennessee. The Alabama Conference of Social Work was not specifically dedicated to race relations, but its composition became biracial; Work presented papers at its meetings and served as a committee chairman in the 1920s and 1930s. Also, Tuskegee sponsored several interracial forums on campus to which southern white college students were invited, and Work usually served as chairman of such meetings. More informal contacts were made when white high school teachers and college professors brought their sociology classes to see the Department of Records and Research.[45]

Some of the groups seeking better race relations were not headquartered in the South, but had numerous southern members. One of these was the American Interracial Seminar in New York City. Its national committee included Jane Addams, Mary McLeod Bethune, Reinhold Niebuhr, Will Alexander, William Allen White, Oswald Garrison Villard, and Monroe Work among its members. The group sponsored a Seminar on Wheels in 1930, which included Tuskegee Institute in the ten-day itinerary.[46]

Because of his proven research skills, Work was asked to serve on the research committees of such biracial groups as the Social

44. *Survey*, May 20, 1916, clipping in Box 2, Tuskegee Institute Lynching Records, Tuskegee Institute Archives; Work (ed.), *Negro Year Book, 1918–1919*, 117; H. L. Anderton to Work, July 5, 1921, in Box LC26, Moton Papers.

45. James D. Burton to Work, January 21, 1933, Minutes of State Interracial Committee of Alabama (typescript, January 18, 1933), both in "Race Relations, Meetings, Conferences, 1933," James W. May to Work, May 12, 1937, Eugene T. Stromberg to Work, December 2, 1937, both in "Race Relations, Meetings, Conferences, 1937," James Treavor to Work, April 21, 1930, in "Race Relations, Improvement of, 1930," Raper to Work, April 29, 1935, in "Race Relations, Improvement of, 1935," all in Records and Research Files.

46. Herbert C. Herring to Work, September 19, 1930, *The American Interracial Seminar* (printed brochure, n.d.), both in "Race Relations, Improvement of, 1930," Records and Research Files.

Science Research Council, the Southern Sociological Society, and the National International Conference, which was chaired by Graham R. Taylor.[47] Will Alexander was responsible for Work's membership on the Advisory Committee on Interracial Relations of the Social Science Research Council. The council, founded about 1926 by Beardsley Ruml, brought together social scientists from various disciplines to coordinate commissions to study specific aspects of American life. Ruml decided to name laymen to chair each commission and asked Alexander to head the one on race relations. One of Alexander's earliest suggestions was to include black scholars. Charles Johnson of Fisk University and Monroe Work were selected in time to attend the first meeting at Dartmouth College. There they were reminded that prejudice did not cease above the Mason-Dixon Line, as Alexander later noted:

> To our utter amazement, we discovered that at the Hanover Inn, in Dartmouth, we had a race problem. The inn was as embarrassed to have those Negroes around as Antoine's in New Orleans would have been. They finally let them come into the dining room but seated them in the corner at a table by themselves. John Mark Glenn, for many years head of the Russell Sage Foundation and a southerner, noticed this dining room arrangement, and he took steps to see that each of those Negro fellows was invited to somebody's table the next evening. We broke that segregation up before it got started, and we had no more difficulty.[48]

Work's skills were also widely utilized by such diverse groups as the Chicago Commission on Race Relations and the National Urban League. He served on numerous advisory boards, including the Advisory Council on Negro Work of the National Child Welfare Association and a committee set up to prepare a series of radio broadcasts on the participation of blacks in American life, sponsored by the United States Office of Education. In addition to his

47. Charles E. Merriam to Work, November 19, 1926, in "Researches Being Made, 1936," Memorandum of Research Committee, 1929, in "Social Conditions, Improvements, 1929," both in Records and Research Files; Alexander to Work, December 28, 1926, in Box 1, Mary von Kleeck to Work, March 26, 1927, in Box 2, both in Work Papers.

48. Dykeman and Stokely, *Seeds of Change*, 181.

time and talents, Work contributed money to such groups as the CIC and the American Civil Liberties Union.[49]

Perhaps as important to the cause of increased understanding between the races was Work's involvement in such predominantly white professional organizations as the American Historical Association, the American Sociological Society, the American Academy of Political and Social Science, the American Economic Association, and the Southern Historical Association. These affiliations placed Work in contact with most of the leading scholars of his day, and he corresponded with a number of them, including such prominent scholars of southern history as Fletcher Green, Thomas P. Abernathy, and Avery Craven.[50]

It may be that Work was accepted by white groups as a kind of token black, but even if this were so, blacks could have been represented by far worse individuals. He provided whites with a living example of an intelligent and capable black. There were several ingredients that made Work an effective force in interracial contacts. His scholarly demeanor and connection with Tuskegee helped to quell resentment over the harsh facts he sometimes presented. He also praised signs of progress and projected an optimism for the future. The Alabama YMCA interracial secretary complimented a speech by Work in 1921, writing, "Instead of grumbling about past conditions, you seemed to look to the future with optimism." Such an approach may be called accommodationism, but Work believed that rewarding efforts and providing hope were effective tools to stimulate more reform.[51]

By employing such devices he did not become an "Uncle Tom." Monroe Work continued to state the truth as he saw it, and by no means did he always say what whites wanted to hear. For example, in 1935 the Board of Missions of the Methodist Episcopal Church,

49. J. W. Studebaker to Work, June 5, 1941, in Box 2, Work Papers; Alexander to Work, January 15, 1929, in "Race Relations, Improvement of, 1930," B. W. Huebsch to Work, August 9, 1932, in "Race Relations, Improvement of, 1932," both in Records and Research Files.

50. Fletcher Green to Work, December 30, 1937, Thomas P. Abernathy to Work, December 31, 1937, both in Box 1, Avery Craven to Work, November 24, 1942, in Box 2, all in Work Papers.

51. Anderton to Work, July 5, 1921, in Box LC26, Moton Papers.

South, asked him to comment on a proposed unit of study for children on the American Negro. The activities included visits to black churches and schools, studying the contributions of blacks, making gifts to black children and needy families, and learning black songs, poetry, and games. Although he praised the goals of the program, Work pointed out deficiencies. He suggested more emphasis be placed upon "what the whites have not done for the Negro, what activities the whites and Negroes do not perform cooperatively, and what the whites have done to themselves in their efforts to maintain an undemocratic democracy." He cautioned that white children should "also learn that the assumption of a paternalistic attitude toward Negroes, or any other racial group, is not conducive to the development of wholesome group relations; in fact, it is definitely injurious to the development and functioning of personality, both for those who adopt the attitude and for whom such an attitude is directed." It was valuable for the children to visit black institutions, Work noted, but "the white child must soon learn that these unnatural, artificial, often superficial and strained interracial cooperative efforts would be unnecessary if the several racial groups were permitted to participate as citizens without regard to race or color in the civic life of the community, be it small or large." In conclusion, he warned against the implications of the terms *Negro poetry* and *Negro music* and asked, "Is there any such thing as a Negro game?" Answering his own question, he wrote, "In my opinion the Negro child and the white child of similar economic and social status tend to play the same, or similar, games."[52]

The scope and extent of his activities highlight not only Work's energy and dedication but also the vast network of interracial contacts available in the 1920s and 1930s. The South has always had its "forgotten alternatives" and voices challenging the region's racial solutions. Too often these have been obscured by the emphasis on the antebellum emergence of proslavery thought, the capitulation to Jim Crow at the turn of the century, and the rise of massive resistance in the 1950s. The interracial activities of Work's day did

52. Work to Constance Rumbough, October 29, 1935, in "Race Relations, Improvement of, 1935," Records and Research Files.

Lithograph of Monroe Work

not represent majority opinion and did not succeed in remaking the South. Nevertheless, ignoring them neglects a valuable southern heritage and prevents true understanding of the Tuskegee program. In the context of the times, faith in the power of such programs was not as absurd as it may appear in historical hindsight.

Monroe Work did not limit his quiet crusading to health programs, antilynching campaigns, and interracial cooperation. Few aspects of the black experience escaped his attention. Keenly believing in the value of "the life of an individual Negro," he felt nothing was too trivial or too great for him to tackle. For example, in 1915 he discovered an advertisement for "little chocolate nigger babies" in the Sears, Roebuck catalog. Julius Rosenwald, who headed that company, was also a trustee of Tuskegee Institute, and so Work suggested that Washington mention the affront to him. Both the principal and Emmett J. Scott emphatically rejected the proposal.[53]

53. Work to Emmett J. Scott, Scott to Work, July 16, 1915, both in Box 664, Washington Papers.

This request was only one of a multitude of suggestions Work showered on principals and other staff members at Tuskegee. In numerous ways his was a quiet but persistent voice for bolder stands and decisive action. Probably realizing that his own influence was more limited than Washington's or Moton's, he promptly notified them whenever a situation arose that he believed needed attention. In 1918 he sent Moton a copy of a labor card issued in Macon County and noted that he understood that "the rule is being enforced that Negro men and women are not to come to town (Tuskegee) without this card." A few years later Work discovered a pattern of declining black voter registration in the county and suggested that Moton take some action.[54]

The plight of individual blacks concerned Work, too. In 1910, for example, he made an appeal for a girl who had been suspended from school, describing her situation.

> She is working in my family for the summer. She is a very poor girl. Her mother is dead and her father does not give her any assistance. In fact, he drew the wages that she earned last summer, and did not give her any support during the past school term. Mrs. Work gave her enough money in April to buy her a dress. She did not enter until December, and had only one book, a grammar.
> I think with what assistance we can give her that she will do much better than she has done. If you will permit her to come back, I will see that she is provided with books.[55]

Work worried about the problems of lower-class, ignorant blacks perhaps more than those of any other group. He realized their vulnerability but also their basic dignity. His attitude toward this kind of people was keenly remembered almost fifty years later by Eunice Rivers Laurie. After she had conscientiously nursed his wife, Work recommended her for the position of public health nurse in the federal syphilis treatment program in Macon County, which later degenerated into the scandalous study of untreated syphilis in black males. How much Work knew about the evolution of this

54. Work to Moton, October 3, 1918, in Box LC13, March 27, 1920, in Box LC22, both in Moton Papers.
55. Work to the Executive Council, July 19, 1910, in Box 604, Washington Papers.

program is unclear, but Laurie remembered his deep interest in her patients and his constant admonishment to be certain they understood what she was saying. "Don't use big words," he would tell her. "Remember you didn't know those words until you came to Tuskegee." He would then continue, "You are no better than they are, just because you know big words. You had the opportunity they didn't have."[56]

Some black and white crusaders engaged in noisy battles for such principles as civil rights, justice, and fairness. Monroe Work quietly devoted his life to changing the fact that "little value was placed on the life of an individual Negro."

56. Eunice Rivers Laurie, my interview, January 7, 1982.

Conclusion / One Firm Pillar

In 1938 Monroe Work was seventy-two years old. He had labored at Tuskegee Institute for thirty years to create a better world. That year he decided to retire from his official duties, and Ralph Davis became the head of the Department of Records and Research. As early as 1925 an editorial in *Opportunity*, the publication of the National Urban League, had noted: "The structure of inter-racial work has one firm pillar in the patient and undemonstrative researches of Monroe N. Work, Editor of the Negro Year Book, to which source many thousands owe their balanced judgments on the race question."[1]

The pillar was not lost with Work's retirement. His quiet crusade continued almost up to the moment of his death on May 2, 1945. Given an office in the library upon retirement, he worked in it daily on an expansion of his bibliography. A great deal of material had been published since 1928, and he hoped to update and revise his original book before his death. The new publication was to be entitled "Bibliography of European Colonization and the Resulting Contacts of Peoples, Races, and Cultures." He intended to place the problems of blacks into a worldwide perspective and to approach the subject from the viewpoint of the effects of European colonization on all races, including the peoples of Africa and Asia, as well as the American Indians and Afro-Americans. By the time of his death, he had completed the outline and had compiled more than seventy-five thousand references.[2]

1. *Opportunity*, January, 1925 (Clipping in Box 1, Monroe Nathan Work Papers, Tuskegee Institute Archives).
2. Jessie P. Guzman, my interview, January 6, 1982.

Although this project consumed most of Work's last years, he continued to be active in interracial affairs and to play an important role at Tuskegee. He attended biracial conferences, read papers, and published articles. Those who were charged with continuing his projects, such as the yearbook and lynching reports, still submitted their results to him for approval. He served on committees that directed school activities, and President Frederick D. Patterson, who had assumed Moton's duties in 1932, later recalled Work's impassioned campaign to preserve Tuskegee's nurse training program when its dismantlement was proposed in 1940. To the very end, Work lived up to his name, never shirking a job he thought needed to be done.[3]

At his death in 1945, Work was survived not only by his wife and friends, but by the results of his faith and his dreams. Before his death he witnessed the continuing financial and educational progress of his people and their new self-confidence and pride. He observed the virtual end of the evil of lynching and saw black life expectancy surpass his most optimistic hope. He watched with interest the small but growing number of dedicated white southern liberals. Only two major tasks were left unfinished. One was the completion of his new bibliography, and the other was the total acceptance by white Americans of the value and significance of blacks as citizens and human beings.

Two elements that characterized Work as a man were his deep love for and pride in his race and his boundless energy to labor in its behalf. The volume of his efforts makes one wonder if there are really only twenty-four hours in a day. Although he did not begin his career until he was in his thirties, in forty-three years he issued sixty-six lynching reports, edited nine editions of the *Negro Year Book*, produced the massive *Bibliography of the Negro in Africa and America*, organized seventeen Negro health weeks, published more than seventy articles, participated in dozens of interracial meetings and organizations, directed the study of sociology at Tuskegee, and filled more than thirty filing cabinets with valuable information on blacks.

3. F. D. Patterson, "Monroe N. Work, Funeral Services, May 4, 1945" (Typescript in Box 1, Work Papers).

His achievements are even more remarkable when one remembers that Work was hired by Tuskegee primarily to keep a record of its graduates. He was a man of vision who recognized and utilized every opportunity to fulfill his dreams. Thus, information gathered for Booker T. Washington's speeches became the nucleus of a massive collection of materials on the Negro; a pamphlet-size document grew into the *Negro Year Book*; a lynching report sent to one newspaper became the most widely recognized authority; one Welfares Day of the annual Tuskegee Negro Conference developed into a nationwide health movement; and the bibliographic sections of the yearbook were expanded into a remarkable book.

His accomplishments received some recognition before his death. Because of his varied contributions to black studies and welfare, Work's biography was included in such social and professional registers as the *International Blue Book, Who's Who in America, Who's Who in American Education, Who's Who in Colored America,* and *Who's Who in the Western Hemisphere.* In 1929, the governor and legislature of North Carolina invited him to visit his native state during Homecoming Week to participate in his county's celebration and to attend the dedication of the North Carolina State Fair. That same year Work was selected by the Harmon Foundation of New York as the Afro-American who had contributed the most creative work to the field of education. He was presented the William E. Harmon first-place gold medal and awarded four hundred dollars in recognition of "scholarly research and educational publicity through his periodic compilation and publication of the *Negro Year Book* and his recent exhaustive *Bibliography of the Negro in Africa and America*."[4]

For his postgraduate accomplishments, the Alumni Association of the University of Chicago gave him its Citation for Public Service at the university's fiftieth anniversary celebration in 1942. Honored for "unselfish and effective service to the community, the nation and humanity" and for exercising "leadership in those civic, social and religious activities essential to a democracy," he was the

4. Jessie P. Guzman, "Monroe Nathan Work and His Contributions," *Journal of Negro History*, XXXIV (October, 1949), 457; Program of Harmon Award Presentation, in Box 1, Work Papers.

(Left) Harmon Award Medal presented to Work in 1928

(Below) Work receiving his honorary degree at Howard University, June 4, 1943

first black to receive the award. The next year, the honorary doctor of letters degree was conferred upon Work at the June commencement of Howard University.[5]

These honors indicate that Work's endeavors were recognized, at least to a small extent, during his lifetime. Yet he became a virtually unknown figure after his death. The scholarly nature of his

5. John Nierveen, Jr., to Monroe Work, May 28, 1942, James M. Nabrit, Jr., to Work, August 26, 1943, both in Box 1, Work Papers.

work and his unassuming personality were undoubtedly two causes. His affiliation with Tuskegee Institute also probably contributed to his neglect, as that school became an object of contempt for many later twentieth century scholars. Some facets of Washington's overall program may deserve scorn, but the positive impact of his school and of people like Monroe Work should be remembered.

Work was truly a pioneer in several areas. The nature and extent of his African interest foreshadowed by several decades current scholarship regarding that continent. Other blacks were interested in Africa in the early twentieth century; Booker T. Washington regarded it as a mission field and W. E. B. Du Bois campaigned for pan-Africanism. Few, however, stressed the importance and the value of the African heritage for Afro-Americans as early as Work did.

Thus, in a way Work was also a father of the "black is beautiful" movement. Fully realizing the problems and weaknesses of his generation of blacks, he nonetheless emphasized pride in his race to a rare extent. He did not merely rely on accounts of black heroes and heroines who had succeeded by white standards; he also recounted the beauty and nobility of the masses. The sacrifices of black washerwomen to educate their children were as significant to him as the accomplishments of the black elite.

Not content with chronicling black progress and decrying the barriers to it, Work pioneered in the attacks on two of the major obstacles to black advancement—poor health and lynching. Although he was not singly responsible for either the increased black life expectancy or the decreased number of lynchings, he made significant contributions in both areas. He was a prime mover in the establishment of National Negro Health Week, which not only coordinated and expanded the earlier sporadic public health campaigns for blacks but also gained the support of the federal government in the crusade to an unprecedented degree. His lynching statistics were the first to be widely distributed in the South and remained the source of most editorial comments on the evil. The CIC and the ASWPL distributed thousands of pieces of literature, but none reached as many people as the editorials in hundreds of newspapers based on the Tuskegee Lynching Report. More interested in bringing improvement than in winning recognition, Work quietly aided other movements as well.

In addition, Work provided one of the first and most persistent voices for increased political activism on the part of Tuskegee Institute. As early as 1920 he suggested that the school "make some effort to increase" the number of black registered voters in Macon County. It is probably not entirely coincidental that the organization in which he had played a prominent role was later transformed into the Tuskegee Civic Association largely through the efforts of two men in the sociology department—Charles Gomillion and Lewis A. Jones. That group launched a campaign that brought federal court rulings aiding the registration of blacks. Eventually the black majority in Macon County came to have the majority voice in its government.[6]

With the same retiring manner that characterized his other efforts, Work labored hardest at providing other scholars with the tools for waging battle against erroneous stereotypes and unjustified discrimination. He considered his greatest contributions to be his bibliography, the *Negro Year Book*, and the files of the Department of Records and Research. All three can be criticized by later standards. The yearbooks and the bibliography contained errors of omission and compilation, and Work's methods of preserving information would horrify most trained archivists. Nevertheless, all three were and still are needed and valuable tools in the search for truth. Many scholars cite Work; few recognize his importance.

Aside from his pioneering efforts and his priceless legacies to scholarship, Monroe Work is significant for the insights his life provides into the age in which he lived. Those years resulted in a tragic and irredeemable waste of human potential. Although the efforts made to combat the conditions prevalent during that time illustrate the indestructability of the human spirit, the talents of too many people were exhausted defending what should have been

6. Work to Robert R. Moton, March 27, 1920, in Box LC22, Robert Russa Moton Papers, Tuskegee Institute Archives; Alabama Center for Higher Education, Statewide Oral History Project (Transcriptions of Interviews, in Tuskegee Institute Archives), Vol. III, No. 042, p. 6.

obvious—the humanity of blacks. Black scholars were forced to become "race men" in the face of the failures of white scholarship. That diversion of talent is a cost of racism that should never be forgotten.

The dilemma Work encountered was similar to that of other black intellectuals at the turn of the century. Those who recognized their importance as part of the Talented Tenth could not freely use their abilities for mere personal advancement. They had a special destiny as agents for the elevation of their fellow blacks. Even those who so desired could not be simply scholars, poets, or scientists; they were Negro scholars, Negro poets, and Negro scientists.

Those blacks with an especially keen sense of responsibility faced a further dilemma. How could they, as individuals, make the most impact? For some, the answer was to move north where they could freely speak out against the evils of discrimination and not be forced to accommodate themselves to southern racial patterns. For others, such as Monroe Work, however, the answer was different. They felt compelled to go where they perceived the need to be the greatest, where the largest number of blacks were being most exploited. To accomplish anything in the South, they had to temper their words and acquiesce in humiliating rituals. The price some paid was high—scorn from other blacks and neglect by later scholars. They were labeled "Uncle Toms" by succeeding generations of southern blacks, who could afford to be more militant partly because of the foundations laid by their forebears.

Work's generation was not guiltless; its members made mistakes. Some continued to practice outmoded patterns of race relations long after their usefulness was past. Others exploited their position for personal gain. Many leaders, both north and south, wasted precious energy bickering among themselves. Monroe Work is an example of his generation's strengths and its weaknesses.

Considering all he accomplished after a late start and facing many obstacles, Work's abilities were obviously considerable. But apart from the research tools he provided others, his scholarly accomplishments were meager. Although many of his articles displayed keen insight, it was others who would popularize his ideas. To some extent, the problem arose from his desire to let the facts speak for themselves; he believed raw data was less likely to be challenged than analysis. He also spread himself too thin, assuring that he would never become a recognized leader in any field. The diffuseness of his efforts was partly due to his belief in the inter-relatedness of social phenomena and partly to his affiliation with Tuskegee Institute, where every staff member was expected to do the work of several people. No one will ever know what he could have accomplished without these limits and the compulsion to be a "race man."

The offer of a job in Oklahoma suggests that Work did not have to return to the deep South and face the conditions from which his father had fled. His ties with Du Bois and with Richard R. Wright, Jr., probably influenced his decision to go to Savannah, but his sense of racial responsibility, nurtured in the social gospel environ-ment at Chicago, was surely the decisive factor. After he arrived in Savannah, he quickly assumed a leadership role in prodding the black elite to action. His ties with Du Bois deepened and he be-came a member of the Niagara Movement. For a while he could have faith in Du Bois' anti-Washington platform, but 1906 brought many rude shocks. Savannah blacks did everything Du Bois pro-posed but were impotent against the rising tide of racism. As Work watched the Sunday Men's Club and the Niagara Movement falter, Booker T. Washington's offer came and seemed to provide the best opportunity for implementing Work's faith in the "impact of fact."

At the crossroads he made a decision. He did not become a dif-ferent man; he merely took a different path. Certainly he was pro-foundly influenced by Washington and Tuskegee, as his later fail-ure to cooperate successfully with Du Bois indicates. On the other hand, he also subtly altered Tuskegee. He became a quiet but per-sistent voice for growth and change, without forsaking the basic principles of the Tuskegee idea. His heart as well as his body be-came committed to the institute.

The focus of later scholars on the shortcomings of Washington and Tuskegee has obscured their successes, but they were obvious to Work. He witnessed and became a part of Tuskegee's pioneering efforts in educating black farmers, improving health conditions, drawing attention to the barbarity of lynching, and aiding southern white liberals in their fight for justice. In hindsight, he may have placed too much faith in the power of such actions. By the time of his death in 1945, other alternatives had become available, but he was an old man and had taken his stand. He did not live to see the maturing political power of urban blacks, the growing activism of the federal government against racial discrimination, or the mobilization of the masses by Martin Luther King, Jr., and others. Being a sociologist does not necessarily make one a seer.

His evangelical assertion that "the truth shall set us free" may have been naïve. Knowledge does not always decrease prejudice. Yet if learning does not tend to create better people, then a lot of effort and public revenues are wasted in trying to instill more than basic literacy in the general population. Mere recognition of problems does not solve them, but until they are recognized, how can they be solved? Monroe Work did not pretend to have all the answers; he only utilized his specific abilities as he saw best in the overall struggle of Afro-Americans.

He was not alone. There were many quiet crusaders who are now ignored. They were people who chose the South and did what they could within the limits that existed during the nadir period of Afro-American history. As human beings they made mistakes, but like Work, not all of them deserve the facile label of "Uncle Tom." Southern blacks, and everyone else, need to recognize the rich heritage of sacrifice by these men and women. They are a part of the rock from which the civil rights movement was hewn.

Index

149